I0187544

"You Don't Want to Go For a Ride"

Our Family's Journey with Autism

JOHN M. HARPSTER

&

TAMARA HARPSTER

Shell Creek
Publishing

Shell Creek Publishing

Lakeside, CA

Copyright © 2017 John M. Harpster and Tamara S. Harpster

All rights reserved. Except as permitted under the U.S. Copyright Act of 1976, no part of this publication may be reproduced, distributed or transmitted in any form or by any means, or stored in a database or retrieval system, without the prior written permission of the publisher.

John M. Harpster and Tamara S. Harpster
Lakeside, CA
Visit our website at www.shellcreekpublishing.com.

ISBN-10: 0-9916109-4-6
ISBN-13: 978-0-9916109-4-5

LEGO® is a trademark of the LEGO Group of companies which does not sponsor, authorize or endorse this book.
LEGOLAND® is a trademark of the LEGO Group of companies which does not sponsor, authorize or endorse this book.
Printed in the United States of America

Front and back cover images provided John T. Harpster

Interior Pictures by John T. Harpster

Book Cover Design by Tamara Harpster
Book Internal Design by Tamara Harpster using Book Formatting template by Derek Murphy @Creativindie
Editing by Tom Laurin, Lee Malin, Sarah De Souza, John M. Harpster and Tamara Harpster
First Edition: (September 2017)

10 9 8 7 6 5 4 3 2 1

Neither the publisher nor the author is engaged in rendering professional advice or services to the individual reader. The ideas, procedures and suggestions contained in this book are not intended as a substitute for consulting with your physician. All matters regarding your health require medical supervision. Neither the author nor the publisher shall be liable or responsible for any loss or damage allegedly arising from any information or suggestion in this book.

While the author has made every effort to provide accurate telephone numbers, Internet addresses and other contact information at the time of publication, neither the publisher nor the author assumes any responsibility for errors or for changes that occur after publication. Further, the publisher does not have any control over and does not assume any responsibility for author or third-party websites or their content.

Preface

This book describes our family's journey through the world of autism. My husband and I have collaborated to capture our memories of raising our son, John-John, while learning how to deal with autism. We started in the 1990s, before widespread Internet access and when autism was still viewed as a lifelong disability that needed to be cured. Over the last twenty-seven years, we have seen the view of autism change. During that time our parenting has also changed. A friend suggested that our story might be interesting and provide insight to other families. This has been a difficult project for us because we are normally private people. However, during our last three years' work on this book, I have found many stories from other families and autistic adults that have helped our family.

We offer no solutions, but we do hope that sharing our experiences might help others understand the challenges for a family that is living with autism. The chapters in the book each contain three sections: my husband's memories, my memories, and a section with resources, references and reflections. The resources and references section of the book contains material we quoted or found helpful, and actions we might change now that we know more about autism. Each chapter reflects our perspective on each situation, including our memories of family life that other parents might also have experienced.

John-John was born in the early '90s and, at the time, it was difficult to find information on autism. The Internet only existed in a few places and the rise in the number of autism cases had just begun to gain media attention. At that time, a diagnosis of autism included a recommendation for institutionalizing the child at some time in the future. We didn't find that acceptable and decided instead to work on ways to reach our child. Unfortunately, many parents were willing to grasp at anything sounding even remotely like a "cure", since standard medicine and psychology did not provide any answers. At the same time, doctors and schools worked to cope with the apparent increase in the diagnosis of autism, and with children who continued living at home. Our early experiences with professionals and my own experience growing up did not give us much confidence in normal institutions, so our family chose an alternate path to try to help our son.

Because it was so hard to find information in the '90s and because of my own issues, I chose to perform my own research on the subject. Based on my discoveries, our family chose not to utilize public schools and professional therapies. Our story does not include descriptions of applied behavior analysis (ABA) therapy, speech therapy and other practices that parents now take for granted. This was not an easy decision and in some ways it would have been simpler to follow the well-defined routine of working with public schools, advocating for John-John and fighting to obtain services for him. We would have been considered good parents who tried their best and, if it didn't work out, it would not be our fault because we had followed the recommended practices of the ranking professionals of the time.

However, when John-John was young, there was not a great deal of evidence that their approach would work and our family would have to live with whatever choices were made. Since we took on the responsibility, we wanted to make the decisions based on what we felt was best for our son. After our early years with him, we chose to homeschool and work with him ourselves. The few success stories I found about autistic children who had become independent autistic adults included a lot of parental involvement. We felt that homeschooling John-John would provide the best opportunity to reach him.

Our decision was also based on my experiences as a child and the social difficulties I had to deal with in school. I remembered my early difficulties all too well, and I did not want to see my child bullied and tormented as I had been in school. Only recently have I finally found some closure to my mental wounds from childhood. When I was younger, I could not see the benefit of subjecting John-John–and my family–to the experimentations that various methods for "curing" autism presented, while the professionals who prescribed them could walk away from their work at the end of the day.

My husband and I felt that if we were to raise our child, we should commit our time and energy to work with him, and not expect others to fix things. Our life together has been challenging due to the choices we made, but we also feel that we gave him the best options we could, considering the information available at the time. Based on the initial assessment, he has come much further than was originally expected. We all continue to work toward the goal of independent living for him at some point. While his social progress has been slow compared to his peers, he has always made progress. My husband and I are very proud of how he has found ways to cope with his challenges.

The story that follows is about our family's experience on the less-traveled road of homeschooling an autistic child. We do not offer a blueprint for curing the condition, but our stories reveal how we have learned to make it through each day with less anger, occasional tears and a lot of humor. Every now and then, we also have those wonderful days when everything goes right and we all see the bright potential of the future. There are many aspects to the autism spectrum—and our story is just one of them. The path we took is not one I would recommend for all parents and there are times that I wish I had been more comfortable with reaching out for help. I hope that our stories will spark ideas for other parents and caregivers for autistic children, just as the books I read helped me when my son was a toddler. New ideas sometimes come from unexpected sources.

I believe that most people on the autism spectrum can communicate. The challenge for the family is to figure out how to find that connection. If every autistic individual could find a way to connect with other people—through hand gestures, special language, repeating scripts, singing or the like–I feel that our world would find new viewpoints that could help all of us. I sincerely hope that sharing our stories helps other families with their autistic child.

Tamara S. Harpster

Foreword

(The following is a note from Tamara's mother. It offers yet another point of view regarding her grandson's potential. Though Tamara's parents lived a great distance from us, it was important to her mother to connect with her grandchildren, and she would make time to visit us as often as possible to build that connection.)

Long before my grandson, John Harpster, was born, I had come to believe that there were children who were a little "different"—myself included. I wasn't autistic, but I had always felt that there was something about me that was a bit out of the ordinary. I don't believe that there's a standard formula of behavior for all of us, therefore, I had no problem relating to   John-John, or J.T., as some family members refer to him. There was just some difficulty through the years in trying to understand where he was coming from. I have learned a lot about autistic children, thanks to J.T., but there is still so much more to master.

One of J.T.'s first activities involved his artistic ability. Little did I realize at the time that he would soon use pictures to communicate with us. What amazed me was a certain picture he had drawn: He was still only five years old, so the thing that most surprised me was how well he drew the men—they were very detailed. I'd seen pictures that other five-year-olds had drawn and a good "stick figure" was about as good as they were able to achieve. I did find out later that J.T. had copied another picture he'd seen, but I still figured since he had drawn it from memory that the picture was very good.

Another pleasant memory occurred when I visited J.T. right after he had moved back to San Diego. Unfortunately, it was cold and rainy for most of the trip. I had never seen the weather that harsh in that part of the country whenever I visited J.T. for his birthday in early February. As a result, he had to play inside and–fortunately for me–he was pretty adept on his computer at the age of six. But I did need to sit with him, and he worked mostly on learning programs. I was very impressed with what he could do. Also during that visit, I would mention that it was time for him to be potty-trained, and though he wasn't successful in mastering that skill during my stay, his mother told me that he was successful in the next week or so. I hope that I did help a little in that regard.

I can't remember if it was the next visit with J.T. or the one after, but I do remember him talking a lot more. He was using pictures to help him communicate and I was very impressed. He had gone through reams of paper to draw hundreds of pictures in an effort to reach out to everyone. Since his thoughts were in those pictures, he would use them to get his message across to people. There is a lot more information about how an autistic person sees the world and connects with it, but I shall leave it up to his parents to explain what they have learned through the years.

"You Don't Want to Go For a Ride"

I will add that as the years went by, I learned a lot about autism and achieved a better understanding of how to identify with my oldest grandson. Every time I went to visit (usually on his birthday), I noticed that he had learned more, which has always been my gauge for success. No matter how much or how little he has gained, I always see it as a plus. I can only assume that, as he gets older, he will continue to astound me with what he has mastered since our last visit.

J.T.'s Nana

Acknowledgements

During the process of writing this book, we have had a lot of help from many different people. We'd like to acknowledge them here. They helped us write a better story.

Lee and Minnie Malin – For suggesting that we write a book and providing support along the way.

Tom and Viv Laurin – For editing and feedback during our long process of creating this book.

The San Diego Autism Society, East County Group – Thank you to the people at this support group, you have helped us find out we aren't so alone in the world.

Sarah DeSouza – For editing help and honest feedback on the book from a woman and mother's perspective. Your input helped to clarify the message we wanted to share.

Annette Stensland – For your support over the years and your bond with J.T., who loves his Nana very much.

Dedication

I dedicate this book to my husband, whose example has helped me to be a better person, and to my son, John-John, who has been my teacher in so many ways over the years. I don't know what I would do without them.

Tamara

To my family, Tammy and J.T.

John

Introduction

There is a fourteen-year age difference between my wife, Tamara, and I. I always thought that if I could have met her when I was sixteen, I could have raised her to do what I say once in a while, but that was not to be. Our age difference and the fact that we met when I was in my thirties did give me a chance to sow some wild oats before I got married... Okay, so my oats were never that wild, but I did get to sow some tame oats before our marriage. Anyway, this story is really not about me, (I'm not autistic) but one day, I did get married, and after a few years of wedded bliss, my son was born. As he grew older, we found out that he was autistic. This story is about him and our family's relationship with him.

Allow me to begin with a little background on my wife, Tammy, and myself. I think a story about an autistic child would not be complete without some information about the parents. After all, autism is a condition whose origins are still a mystery, so maybe clues can be found from historical information about the parents. Tammy feels that she is on the autism spectrum somewhere, but nobody in our family is an expert on this or any other medical or physical condition. My wife and I are the parents of a child who exhibited symptoms that were diagnosed as autism when he was a toddler and he has continued to behave in ways that are consistent with autism.

We want to share our stories with families who would like to expand their knowledge of autism. One of the things I've learned from my son and Tammy is that the manner in which a person on the autism spectrum perceives the world is often quite different from the way others view things. Sometimes, those on the autistic spectrum have difficulty sorting out the important things in their environment from those that most people consider not so important. When a person on the spectrum pays exclusive attention to issues that most would consider minor, many people can't understand what's happening. Sometimes that leads to conflict. One of the purposes of this book is to show that while there are differences between people on the autism spectrum as opposed to those who are not, the conflicts that occur can usually be smoothed over with patience and understanding. I hope our book helps the reader to better understand autism and its impact on the autistic person and their families.

John M. Harpster

1

The Parents (Us)

John

My name is John Monroe Harpster. I am the father in our little family. I was born in Fort Worth, Texas. My family moved to Arlington when I was three years old and I lived there until I was eighteen. My father, John Thomas Harpster, worked at and retired from General Dynamics in Fort Worth after nearly thirty years of service. My parents had two sons and two daughters. Mom and Dad both smoked cigarettes, and eventually my father died of lung cancer. Smoking didn't seem to affect my mother as much, as she lived into her 90s.

I earned my Bachelor of Science degree in Computer Science from California State University, Northridge. As an undergraduate, I drove a delivery truck for a furniture store to help pay my way through college. Since I had served in the U.S. Navy for four years, I used the GI Bill to help pay living and college expenses, and to augment the salary I received as a delivery driver.

After graduation, I received an offer of employment from a company in Fort Worth. That is where I met and began dating my future wife, Tammy. She was a programmer as well, having received her Bachelor of Science degree in Computing and Information Sciences from Oklahoma State University. She had become educated in what was considered —at the time —a male profession. She is one of the most intelligent people I have ever met. The only person I know who is more intelligent than my wife is her father. He has a Master's degree in Geology.

Tammy is a bit of a tomboy. She wears jeans most of the time. My father asked me once if she ever wore a dress. I think the first time I ever saw her in a dress was at our wedding. She made a beautiful bride. Tammy and I fell in love and after about a year of dating, we were married in Dallas. After a few years, John Thomas Harpster, our son, was born.

Tamara

Okay, now it's my turn: my name is Tamara Harpster. I'm fourteen years younger than John, so there's a bit of an age gap between us. During my grade school and high school years, I constantly felt out of place with regard to most other children. When I was four years old, I asked my father why the other kids didn't like me. As far back as I can remember, I could always tell that I didn't

4

quite fit in with others in my peer group. My dad worked at an oil company and my mom was a stay-at-home mom during the '60s and '70s. My parents believed in a good education for all of their children and I received support in all of my studies, even in supposedly male-oriented areas such as math and science.

During my teen years, my family moved across the country several times. We lived in Oklahoma, Colorado and Texas during my school years. The family moved three times during my junior high and high school years. As a result, I felt even more out of place as I struggled to learn how to relate to each new peer group. It was very frustrating because just as I would start to get acquainted and be comfortable with the other kids, we would move again. I can also see now that I was not a typical teenager because I wanted to do well in my classes. I suspect that this made it more difficult for my desire to make friends with my peers.

The summer before my senior year, after another move, since I had to adjust to another new school, I simply "hunkered down" and did my best to get through the year and the end of high school. When I finally started college, it felt like a release from prison because I didn't have to sit and wait for my classmates to finish their assignments. I could pick and choose the classes I wanted to take, and I wasn't stared at as I walked through the halls. I knew of other college freshmen who suffered from homesickness or partying too much, but for me it became a haven where I could study and be recognized for my work.

I graduated from college in 1985 and met John at my first job in Fort Worth. He was the only single man on our project and I was the only woman. For two rather extreme introverts, it was probably the only way we could have met and gotten to know each other. After a few dates, we both felt an attraction and sealed the deal – not with an engagement ring, but through the joint purchase of an Apple IIe computer. Later in the relationship, we found out from each other that we both had the same thought on the drive home after our purchase: "We can't break up now – I'll lose the computer!"

We announced our engagement on February 14 of 1986, and were married that June. John and I had talked about starting a family, but we decided to wait so we could save some money and figure out where we wanted to be when we grew up. We apparently decided in 1989, because that's when I became pregnant with John-John.

Since that time, I've researched and found studies that indicated our child had a higher chance of having autism because of our age difference. With several factors already in play, I now know that we had a high-percentage chance of having an autistic child, but in 1989 this information was either not well-known or had not yet been discovered. I only knew that I was 26, I wanted a family and I was ready to have a child. The only facts I knew at that time about autism were from watching the movie *Rain Man*. I remember news reports during my pregnancy that there was some concern over the increased number of children born with autism, but I was also sure that it would never happen to us. While I had my issues growing up, I made it through school, graduated college, found a job and got married, so I figured I was normal and that my children would be as well. Over the next few years, however, I would discover more information than I ever cared to know about autism and how it affects families everywhere.

Resources, References and Reflections – Parents and Autism Causes

In the years since I was pregnant with John-John, I have read many articles that gave theories on the causes of autism. I have also found that this search is controversial within the autistic community. An autism cure is questionable at best due to concerns about forcing adults to receive medication or therapy, or that parents will use tests to avoid having children with autism.

However, parents with non-verbal, violent children are quite interested in a cure in order to reduce the negative impacts on their child and their family. In my opinion, the current broad definition of autism causes differences of opinion between autistic people and parents. Based on the definition of autism within the Diagnostic and

Statistical Manual of Mental Disorders, or DSM-5[1], autism denotes the deficits with social communication and interaction. The severity can range from a verbal person who misunderstands many social situations to someone who cannot speak and is unable to read social cues. Spoken language is an important part of so many social situations that when a person is unable to speak, it can become challenging to try to find a different way to communicate. For parents who have not experienced autistic people, and whose only knowledge of the spectrum is from the movie *Rain Man*, the lack of verbal communication can seem like a brick wall between them and a relationship with their child. Parents may fear that their child will never be able to live on his or her own, go to school, fall in love or build a family of their own. This fear can drive them to try to solve the problem by attempting to make their child normal, since it is the only way they know how to relate to their children.

In addition, there are other conditions such as Attention Deficit Disorder (ADD), Attention Deficit Hyperactive Disorder (ADHD), epilepsy, Tourette's syndrome, fragile X syndrome (FXS), Sensory

---

[1] The Diagnostic and Statistical Manual of Mental Disorders, 5th Edition (DSM-5) is a manual used by psychiatrists for the diagnosis of mental disorders. In 1952 the manual was developed from statistical history and other sources to standardize psychiatric diagnosis. The number 5 refers to the version, in this case the fifth version of the DSM. Autism is one of the disorders defined and DSM-5 updated the diagnostic criteria for Autism in 2013. At that time, several separate diagnoses were combined into one set of criteria for a diagnosis of Autism Spectrum Disorder (ASD).

Processing Disorder (SPD), Obsessive Compulsive Disorder (OCD),
and intellectual disability that can coexist with the communication
difficulties of autism and cause additional issues in the autistic
individual. Many individuals and families can learn to accept and deal
with all of these problems, but it is extremely challenging and can
cause a great deal of stress for everyone involved. When most of our
society has families with children that talk, and these families share
stories about their children and their normal lives, the parents of an
autistic child can feel very alone and may wish for a simpler life
without all of the problems of the disorder.

For the autistic individual, all of these conditions are often
viewed as a part of who they are and the core of the personality
because they don't know any other way. To parents and family
members, the conditions are viewed as obstacles to the relationship
they envisioned with their child before the diagnosis. These two very
different views of the same disorder lead to controversy and
disagreement over whether autism should be cured or supported. The
parents want a cure – not because they want to change their child,
but because they want to get to know their child in the only way
with which they are familiar. For autistic people, their
communication problems, stimming[2], anxiety and other elements of

---

[2] Self-stimulatory behavior, also known as stimming and self-stimulation, is
the repetition of physical movements, sounds, or repetitive movement of objects

their lives are a part of them, and so a cure would mean that other people cannot love them as they are.

There are many theories about the causes of autism, but there is not yet a consensus on a single cause – or if there even is a single cause, due to the variety of people on the autism spectrum. The viewpoint has transitioned from seeing the cause of autism as a psychological disorder to seeing it as a disorder caused by genetics or environment. Society has moved away from pointing a finger at the parents for their behaviors to blaming the environmental

---

common in individuals with developmental disabilities, but most prevalent in people with autistic spectrum disorders. It is considered a way in which autistic people calm and stimulate themselves. Common stimming behaviors (sometimes called stims) include hand flapping, rocking, head banging, repeating noises or words, snapping fingers, and spinning objects. In the Diagnostic and Statistical Manual of Mental Disorders, published by the American Psychiatric Association, this type of behavior is listed as one of the symptoms of autism or "stereotyped and repetitive motor mannerisms".

Rosalind Bergemann (2013). An Asperger Leader's Guide to Living and Leading Change. Jessica Kingsley Publishers. ISBN 9780857008725.

Valerie Foley (2011). The Autism Experience. ReadHowYouWant.com. ISBN 9781458797285.

Stephen M. Edelson, Ph.D. "Self-Stimulatory Behavior". Autism Research Institute.

Temple Grandin, PhD (November–December 2011). "Why Do Kids with Autism Stim?". Autism Digest. Retrieved 25 March 2014.

Eileen Bailey (27 August 2012). "Stimming". Health Central. Retrieved 25 March 2014.

"Stimming: What autistic people do to feel calmer". BBC. 5 June 2013. Retrieved 25 March 2014.

"Autism Spectrum Disorders", 1994, Diagnostic and Statistical Manual, American Psychiatric Association

contaminants or genetic background for causing autism. In turn, this has led to many researchers looking for a cause that can be prevented. The interest in finding this cause and a possible prevention of autism can be seen on the Internet with more than thirty-six million results from a Google search.

While this is an improvement for parents, autistic adults dislike that their condition is viewed as a disorder, when they feel that it is part of who they are and that some of the accompanying conditions are strengths instead of weaknesses. However, due to the early studies and documentation about autism, a strong negative view still exists in the general populace, as well as an equally strong feeling that autism is something that should always be prevented. The neurodiversity movement has grown, comprised of autistic adults and others with disabilities who seek acceptance of the condition instead of trying to eradicate it. In the meantime, many parents are interested in possible causes and prevention of autism due to the association of difficult behavior and problems in obtaining adequate support for children with the condition.

As someone in the middle of this discussion, I see points on both sides, while being concerned about trying to change autistic behaviors in order to fit a cultural definition of normalcy. I would like to see both sides meet in the middle, where help is provided in communication while recognizing the strengths of an autistic person.

Over the years, I have read about autism and the possible causes as part of my mourning over the family I thought we would have. There was a part of me that felt if I could find something to blame for the difficulties with our son, then the problems could somehow be fixed. I also had to work through my own self-blame and the choices I made that might have made things worse, and life more difficult for him and our family.

For example, as part of my research, I learned that our family shows several areas that may have contributed to an increased likelihood of an autistic child. In our case, one item was John's age as a father. When I gave birth to our son, John had just turned 41. Studies have shown that the risk of autism increases as the father gets older (i.e. above the age of 35 at the time of conception). Since the earliest known study regarding this risk wasn't performed until 1995, we were completely unaware of the increased potential for autism when John-John was born.

The other risk factor comes from my side of the family, many of whom are introverted. Both sides of my family have a strong interest in the scientific fields as well. This has also been linked to higher autism rates. During my research for this book I have come to feel that I am an undiagnosed female with what was known as Asperger's

Syndrome[3]. With these factors and based on current research, John and I had a strong chance of having a child with autism.

The following is a short list of current theories and research in this area. I've included these references because I remember my early search when I was trying to understand what happened and if there was a possibility of having more children with autism. However, this is not an exhaustive list of the causes, and continuing research may refute these ideas in the future, just as the psychological model was overturned. I will also add that there are families who show none of the more solidly supported risk factors for an autistic child who have one, so there is no guarantee that autism will not affect your child. As the years pass, I find it more productive to focus on the strengths of my son, support working through his weaknesses and love him for who he is – not who I wanted him to be. Reviewing the possible causes can help in the grieving process of the loss of the child a parent envisioned, but I don't recommend that the search replace working with and loving the child you have.

---

[3] In the USA, the term Asperger's Syndrome is no longer used in diagnosis and the term Autism Spectrum Disorder (ASD) is now used in the latest edition of the DSM-5. Other countries still use the term Asperger's Syndrome and differentiate it from classical autism. The primary difference between Asperger's Syndrome and classical autism is speech abilities. Children diagnosed with Asperger's Syndrome develop language normally and primarily have issues in reading social cues. Children with classical autism are delayed in speech or do not develop speech in addition to their issues in reading social cues.

Andersson, O. et al. "Effect Of Delayed Versus Early Umbilical Cord Clamping On Neonatal Outcomes and Iron Status at 4 Months: A Randomised Controlled Trial". *BMJ* 343.nov15 1 (2011): d7157-d7157. Web. 23 Mar. 2016.

Carnegie Mellon University. "Genetic risk for autism stems mostly from common genes." ScienceDaily. ScienceDaily, 20 July 2014.

"Key Findings: Population Attributable Fractions for Three Perinatal Risk Factors for Autism Spectrum Disorders, 2002 and 2008 Autism and Developmental Disabilities Monitoring Network". *CDC – Centers for Disease Control and Prevention*. N.p., 2014. Web. 23 Mar. 2016.

Schieve, Laura A. et al. "Population Attributable Fractions for Three Perinatal Risk Factors for Autism Spectrum Disorders, 2002 and 2008 Autism and Developmental Disabilities Monitoring Network." Annals of epidemiology 24.4 (2014): 260–266. PMC. Web. 23 Mar. 2016.

Silberman, Steve. "Neurotribes: The Legacy of Autism and the Future of Neurodiversity". 6th ed. New York: Penguin Random House LLC, 2015. Print.

Wang, Sam. "How to Think About the Risk of Autism". *New York Times* 2015: SR6, New York Edition. Web. 29 Mar. 2014.

2

Pregnancy

John

Our son's story begins in the spring of 1989, when Tammy became pregnant. In 1987 we had moved to San Diego, both found jobs and started saving to buy a home. We had been married for three years and thought it might be time to have a child. I was a bit leery of the idea at first, but we had already had one possible pregnancy a few months earlier when Tammy was late with her period, so I found myself a little excited about the idea of becoming a father. And, Tammy wanted children – preferably a boy and a girl.

Based on John Thomas's birth date, he was conceived sometime in April or May of 1989 and we confirmed in June that Tammy was pregnant. She had been experiencing morning sickness after missing her period, but she thought it was either the stomach flu or stress from her project at work. I had a feeling that she was pregnant and I was excited, but nervous about the whole thing.

It turned out that June 1989 was one of those months that might best be described as stressful when rating one's life events. In the space of thirty days, I was laid off, Tammy confirmed she was pregnant, and we got evicted by our landlord after the house we rented was sold to a new owner. Being laid off turned out to be a good thing, because I didn't really like my job and it turned out to be a relief to be free from that boring atmosphere. The eviction occurred because the new owner wanted to move into the house, so he told us to vacate the premises.

Since we had recently heard gunfire at night in the neighborhood, along with helicopters with their searchlights hovering overhead, it seemed like a good idea to move at the time. Before she became pregnant, Tammy had agreed to work and let me have some time off in return for the break she took when we first moved to San Diego two years earlier. But when she came in smiling to confirm that, yes, she was pregnant, I panicked and wondered how I was going to take care of my family.

That June was certainly a stressful month for me, but in the end everything turned out all right. I ended up finding a better job and we moved to a nicer neighborhood. Our new home was closer to where Tammy and I worked and the added stress of nighttime gunfire had vanished. Early the next year, J.T. was born.

Tammy's pregnancy went as normally as could be expected: morning sickness for a few months, getting bigger and then a lot bigger. We were initially concerned about how big the baby would be, but Tammy seemed to take it all in stride. I figured that it would be easy to care for a baby. Keep him fed, keep him dry and he shouldn't put up much of a fuss. I really wasn't quite sure why Tammy shot me those looks when I told her how things should be, but that's just me.

As Tammy's due date drew nearer, the doctors recommended that they induce labor because of J.T.'s size — before they could implement their decision, her water broke and we wound up in the hospital for a couple of days waiting for her labor to begin. They had given her oxytocin, a drug used to induce labor. In spite of these meds, her labor never really initiated. She finally agreed to a cesarean section, which she was reluctant to go through at first because she had always wanted a natural birth. The doctor eventually told me privately that the baby was just too big for that type of delivery. She resisted the C-section for a few days until it became clear to everyone that the birth was not going to happen without it.

John T. Harpster entered this world at around two o'clock in the morning on February 1, 1990. He had all of his fingers and toes and cried very well, so things seemed all right at that point. Tammy had problems getting around due to soreness from the surgery, but our mothers came out for a few weeks to help us get by. We named our new baby John Thomas, after my father, which made my side of the family very happy. John Thomas Harpster weighed just shy of ten pounds when they finally sliced my wife open and scooped him out of her.

Tamara

In the spring of 1989, I became pregnant, but I didn't quite believe it at first. I had always had a sensitive stomach, so when my morning sickness began, I just figured it was stress due to John's job changes, my job and our neighborhood. When I saw the extra mark on the home-pregnancy test, I still didn't believe it and took another test the next day. When that test showed up positive, I decided it was time to visit the doctor. When I received the confirmation from the doctor's office, I finally believed that I was pregnant.

I still remember telling John. He was in the living room enjoying his time off. He sat on the couch watching TV, and I felt calm and happy. I grinned as I told him, but I was a bit shocked when he didn't react as happily. A few months earlier, we had both been disappointed that I was not pregnant and I thought he would be happy with my news. He mentioned something about needing to find a job, after which I told him that he had a few months and should enjoy his time off. He still gave me this grim look, but he did tell me that he was happy about the pregnancy and only worried about our finances.

In spite of the turmoil, I remember feeling an overwhelming sense of calm as I told him the good news. I felt that everything would work out and that he wouldn't have to hurry back to work, since I still had my job. I felt guilty that he thought he needed to find a job so quickly, since he had worked while I took time off the year before. In spite of my lack of concern, he conducted an employment search and found a job soon after that turned out to be a much better position. It made good use of his talents as a software developer and he actually enjoyed work again.

My pregnancy was uneventful; there were no signs during the doctor visits that something might be wrong with the child I was carrying. I experienced morning sickness for the first trimester and chose to eat very bland foods. I dutifully took multivitamins and worried a bit that I had taken an over-the-counter painkiller before I knew I was pregnant. The doctor told me that the baby was developing just fine, and an ultrasound at four to five months showed that he seemed to be growing nicely. I had an ultrasound due the doctor's concern that I might be pregnant with twins. The ultrasound showed only one fetus who was large for his gestational age. Due to his size, I was also tested for gestational diabetes. The test was negative, the fetus just seemed to be extra-large. At least John waited until after the pregnancy to tell me that large babies were normal on his side of the family. Ten pounds or more would not have been considered out of the ordinary.

We visited both of our families during my second trimester. We went for a ride in his brother's brand-new car, which I thought would be fine until I learned that I wasn't done with morning sickness. When I experienced motion sickness along with it, my stomach reacted accordingly. I spoke up and asked him to pull over – quickly. I was relieved that I threw up outside the car and didn't ruin his back seat.

I did experience one scare during my pregnancy, after I hadn't eaten much during a busy day at work. I came home and, after dinner, threw it all up. I normally had morning sickness in the morning so I was surprised by my loss of dinner that evening. I also thought I was finished with this part of pregnancy since it had been over a week since my last bout, but apparently not. I didn't think much of it, shrugged it off and was glad that I usually lost it once and then was done with it – at least until the next day.

The next morning, John asked, "Do you feel okay? Your eye is red." I said I felt fine and figured I had some red-eye or veins popping. Then I looked in the mirror and the white of my right eye was completely red, which I had never seen before. I quickly made an appointment with the doctor to make sure there wasn't something seriously wrong. I found out that a person can throw up forcefully enough that it can burst blood vessels in your eyes, which causes the iris to turn completely red. Fortunately, I think that was the last time I had morning sickness and I was very glad to be done with that part of my pregnancy. I do know that my mood was very calm throughout most of the pregnancy, which I attribute to the hormones working in synch.

During my eighth month, I had stomach flu and throwing up while eight months pregnant is not a pleasant experience. I was pretty miserable for a couple of days and was very glad that was the only time I got sick while pregnant. Meanwhile, at Christmas, my husband thought that my round stomach looked like Buddha's, so he took pictures of me seated in lotus position with my very pregnant belly sticking out. I think he might have been complimenting me at the time, but now I'm not so sure. And, he did worry about me quite a bit. I remember taking the laundry out to the garage and tripping over the step because I couldn't see around the basket and my belly. Fortunately, I fell onto the basket of soft clothes, so no damage was done, but he scolded me for not asking for help.

My husband's reaction could vary. I recall when I was cooking fish in our toaster oven and it caught fire. I remembered our fire extinguisher, waddled over to retrieve it and I was able to put out the fire. In the meantime, I wondered where my husband was and why he wasn't helping before I nearly burned down our house. I went to the bedroom and told him about the fire in the toaster oven. He shrugged and asked if the fire was out, and went back to watching his TV show. I shook my head and fixed something that didn't involve the risk of fire.

With an uneventful pregnancy, I expected a normal, natural childbirth – especially after having seen my mother's pregnancy with my sister when I was eleven and a half. Unfortunately, I was not mentally prepared for what happened during my own birth experience, so disappointment and postpartum depression occurred after John-John's birth. My depression had an adverse effect on our family over the next few years, as I began adjusting to motherhood while also dealing with my own inner demons. I attempted to reach out for help once or twice after John-John was born, but I was told that being "blue" was normal and I would eventually get over it. The next few years revealed how bad that advice was, so in 1996 I finally admitted that I needed help. I sought professional guidance and obtained relief from my depression. This event marked my first steps to better mental health, which continues to this day.

During those years, I spent a lot of time looking for reasons for my son's autism. I suspected that something was different with my son – even during the pregnancy. I remember that he reacted very strongly during my sonograms. I had two during the pregnancy, due to his size. During the first, he was too small for me to feel very much, but I could sense movement as they pointed the scanner at my belly. For the next two, he would kick and try to move away from wherever the device was pointed and I could definitely feel those movements. When I was first admitted to the hospital, they took one last sonogram to verify his position and how large he had become. During that last exam, I was fairly certain that he was going to kick his way out of my stomach, like the scene from the movie *Alien*. I was very happy when they finally turned the machine off. Since sonograms use high-frequency sound waves, I suspect the noise from the device had caused him pain, and that this was why he tried to move away from it.

John-John was also very active during my pregnancy. He moved and kicked quite a bit. I still have a tender spot on my left side from when I was seven or eight months pregnant. I remember the doctor telling me that babies can kick strongly enough to break a mother's rib, so I was glad that at least I hadn't been kicked quite that hard – but I sure could have done without that sore spot.

Another anomaly I noticed after John-John's birth was that his left ear was very sensitive to pressure. This caused problems during his first week of breastfeeding. He would not allow me to lay him on his left side because it pushed on that ear, so I became somewhat lopsided as he fed from my left side. After a week of this behavior, he allowed me to feed him from both breasts. He is still sensitive in that ear.

My left ear is also sensitive and I have always had sensitive hearing, often to the point of experiencing pain when I hear certain sounds or music. Thankfully, my hearing has become somewhat worse as I've grown older, so I'm not as bothered as I was when I was younger. Hypersensitive hearing is not the benefit that most people believe it is, especially in a world that loves loud, strong, bass tones on high-end speaker systems.

Years later, I found out that his head had been turned to one side during my attempt at labor, which is one reason why my labor did not progress. His position in utero pushed the left side of his head against my pelvic bone when a contraction occurred. I suspect that this added to the sensitivity in his ear, although he does not have the same reaction to certain sounds that I do. I do remember one instance when John-John and I took a walk. We were near an apartment and many children played outside. Several adults were near a truck where people unloaded a large, heavy metallic object. As John-John and I neared, those people dropped the object and it emitted a very loud clanging sound. My son and I both flinched and ducked. I noticed that no one else reacted to the sound even though it was very loud. John-John and I kept walking and I just made a mental note that my son experienced a similar sensitivity to loud noises. [1]

I realize now that these oddities made sense and were indications of sensory problems for him. At the time, they seemed as oddities that I filed away as concerns that one would notice as a worried new mother. I figured that I was worrying too much and so I forgot about them – until later, when he was found to be autistic.

Resources, References, and Reflections –
Pregnancy and Birth

Based on my experiences with my birth and the mental illness I had, I wanted to share resources for other mothers who may be experiencing similar feelings. If the mother is disappointed with her birth experience, no matter what kind of experience she has, she should receive help and support. Many mothers are satisfied with their birth,

---

[1] I still remember a physical I took for my first job; they administered a hearing test for one portion of the exam. I thought the test took a long time and the sounds were very faint, but I kept going and pressed the button when I thought I heard something. When I exited the booth, the doctor looked at me, head tilted at an angle and said, "You have very good hearing." I just shook my head and thought, "Tell me something I don't know." But as usual for me, I didn't say anything.

but for those dealing with depression, anxiety or trauma, some of the resources may aid in finding someone to talk to. Focusing only on physical health ignores the impact that depression, anxiety and trauma can have on the child and the family.

Another reason for this section is my husband asked me if I thought the delay in the delivery of John-John might have contributed to his autism. After many years of thinking about this question, I mostly believe that he would have been autistic no matter what. However, a part of me thinks I did something during my pregnancy – or the delivery – to cause his problems.

After several days of attempting an active labor, I finally had a cesarean section. While growing up, I was often teased and called a boy. Even when I reached college age, I would be called sir and I did not get calls or attention from the young men around me. I lacked self-confidence that I was fully a woman, so it was very important to me to be able to give birth as naturally as possible. I also knew that cesareans involved open abdominal surgery that could lead to complications and poor outcomes for the mother and baby. I felt very strongly that there was a "right" way to have a child and that it did not involve epidurals, episiotomies, confinement to a bed or other interventions. However, because of my low self-esteem and lack of confidence, I did not voice my innermost beliefs, even when I noticed that events had happened that I did not entirely agree with.

I spent several days in the hospital with stalled labor, in spite of the medications the staff had administered. Since they dosed me with a Pitocin drip, I was unable to walk or get much sleep. They also did not allow me to eat during that time because of the possibility of vomiting during surgery. A monitor showed John-John's heartbeat as normal and steady, except when my labor picked up the pace. Based on what I learned later, since he was pushed up against my pelvic bone, the increased contractions would have caused fetal stress and a lower heartbeat. My attempt at labor certainly lasted much longer than is usually allowed in the U.S., but I knew from my family history that lengthy labors were normal, so I didn't think it was that unusual.

Three days after I entered the hospital, I finally accepted the fact that I would not be able to deliver my son on my own and would have to undergo a caesarean section. The memory of that moment still hurts, and I wept bitterly while John held me. It hurt even more when I read my medical record, which merely stated that I was "tearful," with no mention or importance given to my mental state or the sense of failure I would experience from this decision. Later on, I added to my guilt by remembering that some studies show a link between cesareans and an increase in autism diagnoses.

During John-John's early years, an autism diagnosis was considered a grim outcome. I beat myself up for my lack of will and action during the pregnancy and birth process. I have also wondered if my lack of treatment for depression during his first few years contributed to how he turned out. One school of thought tells me that genetics and environmental influences are the main causes, but a part of me does feel a level of guilt – this in spite of Dr. Bernard Rimland's attack of the "refrigerator mother theory"[2] and later research that also points to genetics as the cause of autism.

After many years of blaming myself for my decisions, I had to decide that even if my actions did cause his autism, I can't go back and change what happened. However, I can change how I act today, so I work to better myself and help my son. Based on my struggles, I want to encourage parents who are depressed to seek help for themselves. I took many years to learn the lesson that if I want to take care of others, I must first take care of myself so I don't fail them at a critical point. Don't be ashamed to ask for help and don't be afraid to push for that assistance when others tell you that a problem "isn't that big a deal."

------

[2] When Dr. Leo Kanner performed research in 1943 studying autism, he noted that mothers and fathers seemed to lack warmth towards children exhibiting autistic characteristics. In the 1950s and '60s, Dr. Bruno Bettelheim formally proposed the Refrigerator Mother theory, which was widely accepted by medical experts and the public at the time. In 1964, Dr. Bernard Rimland published *Infantile Autism: The Syndrome and its Implications for a Neural Theory of Behavior,* which attacked the Refrigerator Mother hypothesis. Dr. Bettleheim then published *The Empty Fortress: Infantile Autism and the Birth of Self,* where he compared autism to being a prisoner in a concentration camp with the implication that the parents were the guards and the child the prisoner. Parents of autistic children spoke out against the theory in the 1960s and pushed back against the belief that autistic children had been abused. Dr. Kanner eventually spoke out against the Refrigerator Mother theory and the theory has been widely discarded in the US; however, France and South Korea still believe in this mindset. The current theory is that autism is caused by genetics and is a physical difference instead of an emotional disorder caused by poor parenting.

To those who know a parent who is depressed, don't be afraid to speak up and let them know you support them. Part of the reason I finally sought treatment was due to my husband's backing and acceptance of me. If I had not had that extra little push, it might have been much longer before I sought help – if I ever realized that I needed help at all.

In the end, the parents and the child must live with the choices made for their family–not the doctors, not the therapists, not the teachers, and not the friends or family who invariably offer their well-meaning advice. However, at the end of the day, when the door finally closes and all the advice-givers leave you with your thoughts, the parents and their child will have to live with the behavior and consequences that result from their decisions. I also came to the realization that while I could have taken actions that may have made things better, those acts might very well have made the situation much worse. I did the best I could with what I knew at the time and that will simply have to do.

In the years since John-John's delivery, there continue to be changes and improvements in the birthing process. Even with these resources available, a first-time mother can easily be intimidated by the overwhelming responsibility she feels to nurture a healthy baby. There are many resources for women who are depressed or grieving after their birthing experience, they can still obtain more help than they are currently receiving. These resources are available on the Internet and they look to be quite supportive, so I encourage mothers who feel that they are experiencing depression to seek help as soon as possible. This includes reaching out to your partner, family or friends if you need support to ask for medical help. I know that John's strength made a difference when I sought help for myself.

Postpartum Depression and Birth Trauma

Over the years, studies have shown that many women experience significant depression after childbirth. These symptoms can include feelings of anger, lack of interest in the baby, crying and sadness, and possible thoughts of harming baby or self. Postpartum depression lasts well beyond the typical "baby blues" period that occurs for about a week or so after the birth. Also, a new disorder called birth trauma has displayed characteristics common to post-traumatic stress disorder, or PTSD. In both cases, the mother does not function rationally, and as a result needs help and support. I speak from experience when I talk about not thinking rationally, and I know that these mental illnesses can affect the care of the newborn and any other children in the family.

Both post-partum depression and birth trauma can be difficult for parents to talk about, because there an expectation in US culture that there is a quick recovery from childbirth. Medical professionals may not have the requisite experience in recognizing the signs of depression and trauma. Family and friends who do not have personal knowledge of depression or trauma may not understand how the birth experience can affect the mother, and so are unable to provide help or support. This leaves the mother feeling isolated and unable to move on from the birth experience. While my research points to mothers as the most affected, the birth affects the father and other children as well, so their feelings should not be discounted. The goal should always be to support the family so that everyone is cared for. If the parents receive support and understanding, they will be better able to take care of the new baby.

Support groups can help mothers and fathers so they don't have to deal with these issues on their own. In addition to the resources I have included, I recommend that parents search for their own solutions for the help they need.

Childbirth Loss

After my birth experience, I searched for books that helped explain why I felt so badly about what had happened. I found a few that were written with an angry view point, which validated my feelings but did not help me deal with my anger at what I felt I had lost. The only book I found helpful at the time dealt with mourning losses at childbirth. *Ended Beginnings: Healing Childbearing Losses* provided a sympathetic view with ideas on how to mourn and move on after a loss. The focus is on miscarriages, stillbirths and infant deaths, with mention of other types of loss. I found it very helpful. In my opinion, mothers should be allowed to grieve for the loss of their ideal childbirth so they can let go of the bad experience and move on. Childbirth losses should not be a contest to see who suffered the most horribly, but instead should recognize that each mother needs to express and recognize her feelings so she can better deal with them and find her own personal solution.

Non-Medical View of Birth

The resources in this section focus on a non-medical focused method of birthing. All of the resources recognize the importance of modern medicine in healthy births but also look beyond to some of the mental and spiritual aspects of the mother and the family. I recommend the following books, authors and websites:

Ina May Gaskin is the founder and director of the Farm Midwifery Center. She advocates for positive birth experiences for all women. She has been a midwife since 1971 and has participated in more than 1,200 births. Her center is noted for its low rates of intervention and low mortality rates. She has also contributed to several books for childbirth.

La Leche League International is a group that supports breastfeeding. Mothers can connect with each other at the monthly group meetings, which are run by volunteer leaders who have breastfeeding experience. I know that some women have had negative experiences with groups, but I found their meetings helpful and healing. It was refreshing to see other women with babies and toddlers dealing with some of the same issues I did while I tried to figure out how to be a mother. They also sell many good titles on their website. A toll-free number is available 24 hours a day for questions about breastfeeding. I served as a leader many years ago and I took a nighttime shift for the help line. There may also be a local leader you can call. All leaders are accredited by La Leche League and receive training before they can begin helping mothers. See the reference for La Leche League for more information on how to contact them and their leadership program.

Michel Odent – French obstetrician who set up a clinic focusing on a supportive environment for women nearing childbirth. *Birth Reborn* contains beautiful pictures of women laboring and giving birth. I found these images very powerful and empowering, but be prepared for viewing the human body in its natural form.

Bettelheim, Bruno. *The Empty Fortress*. New York: Free Press, 1967. Print.

"Birth Trauma Association / Helping People Traumatized By Childbirth". *Birthtraumaassociation.org.uk*. N.p., 2016. Web. 23 Mar. 2016.

Gaskin, Ina May. "Home Page". *Ina May Gaskin*. N.p., 2016. Web. 23 Mar. 2016.

Griebenow, Jennifer Jamison. "Healing the Trauma: Entering Motherhood with Post-Traumatic Stress Disorder (PTSD)". *Midwifery Today* 2006. Web.

Kluchar, Jodi. "Did You Have A Traumatic Birth Experience?" *Post-Traumatic Stress Disorder After Childbirth*. N.p., 2016. Web. 23 Mar. 2016.

"LLLI / Home". La Leche League International. N.p., 2016. Web. 23 Mar. 2016.

La Leche League International Website - http://www.llli.org/

La Leche League USA Website and group locator - http://www.lllusa.org/locator/. Call 877-452-4324 for more information or email to info@lllusa.org.

La Leche League Leadership - http://www.llli.org/lad/talll/talll.html - Resources about the accreditation process for a La Leche League Leader.

Leboyer, Frédérick. *Birth without Violence*. New York: Knopf, 1975. Print.

Odent, Michel. (May 12, 1984) *Birth Reborn*. Westminster, Maryland. Pantheon.

Panuthos, Claudia, and Catherine Romeo. *Ended Beginnings*. South Hadley, Mass.: Bergin & Garvey Publishers, 1984. Print.

Rimland, Bernard. *Infantile Autism*. [New York]: Appleton-Century-Crofts, 1964. Print.

3

The First Years

John

We took our new baby home and doted over him. Both of our mothers had come to help for the first week or two. When they went back to their own lives, reality hit us – hard. J.T. required round-the-clock nurturing for quite a while. He cried incessantly when left alone, but he was happy as a clam when we carried him around. That was my job for a long time – carrying him around the house. He was content being toted from room to room and riding in the family car. I guess it was because of the constant motion. When I wasn't lugging him around the house, I was driving him all over town.

At first, J.T. seemed like a normal youngster. He met all of the first-year milestones: smiling at six weeks, rolling over at three months, sitting up and crawling around at four or five months. He was pretty advanced as far as walking was concerned. He took his first steps before nine months, but he had always liked to move anyway. When we first brought him home from the hospital, he tried to roll over and get to all of the interesting things. When he began to walk, his behavior changed, which was a relief for Tammy and myself. He cried less often, now that he was finally able to get around in the outside world as quickly as he wanted.

By the end of his first year, he had learned to talk – but just words, not sentences. His vocabulary was small at first: *Dada* was his first word, but he was sporadic with that one, d*oggy*, because we had a beagle at the time and *pizza*, an important food choice because it looked interesting to him. For some reason, he had not yet said *Mama*. He also didn't babble like other babies. He could say one word at a time, but he mostly didn't try to talk. He was much more interested in moving around, especially when he was able to walk.

Once he began to crawl, he seemed very curious and got into everything. Whenever he found a lower shelf, he would immediately empty it of whatever items were there. He liked outside and crawling to investigate the grass, rocks and other items found in our yard. If anything was left on the floor he immediately had to go and investigate. He also was fascinated with our dog's crate and liked to open and close the door, especially if she was in the crate. He was constantly in motion while he was awake, emptying toy boxes and moving to the next thing that had to be emptied.

During those first years, we noticed several things about him that differed from normal infant behavior. Actually, my mother noticed it first. She had had experience in mothering four of her own, so she mentioned that J.T. would spend time staring off into space. She told us that this was not normal behavior for a child. During these periods of self-absorption, he would not react to anyone who talked to him or called out his name. He would just stare straight ahead, as if transfixed by an object.

At first, my mother entertained the notion that he might be deaf. Then one day while we were visiting her, someone in the kitchen dropped a pan. It hit the floor with a loud crash and J.T. reacted by quickly looking in the direction of the noise. My mom then learned that deafness certainly wasn't the problem. However, we noticed his lack of responsiveness and we adjusted by repeating things several times. One of his nicknames since early childhood has been John-John. Very often he wouldn't respond when we said his name, so we would repeat it a second time later to get his attention. Soon it changed from John-pause-John to John-John, and the nickname stuck.

After Tammy recovered from her Cesarean, she had the option to return to work. She chose instead to stay at home with J.T. She had been employed at a very high-stress position and even before we knew about J.T.'s problems, she felt it important to be home with him. Fortunately, my software job paid well, so we were okay financially, but Tam soon discovered the stress associated with a home life with our son.

These issues raised our family's anxiety level significantly. During the first eighteen months, I would come home from work and Tammy would practically throw him into my arms. Then she would run into the bedroom to take a break from his bouts of frenzy and crying. I would carry him in my arms or drive with him for an hour or so in order to give my wife a break from her daily grind. Our families were thousands of miles away, which seemed fine until we had this child who required so much attention.

We both felt that we needed something different in our life, but weren't quite sure what that should entail. Tammy and I were firmly against leaving J.T. in childcare. We felt that parents who have the financial means should raise their own children. Tammy was prone to bouts of depression, so along with her postpartum symptoms and distress at having a cesarean section instead of a natural delivery, she had a tough time coping with our extremely ill-tempered son.

When J.T. was around a year old, I had a thought: If we bought a small business and ran it together, we could both be around to take care of him. Tammy did not warm to the idea at first, but when I suggested that we could move out of San Diego, she became more interested. She had always wanted to live in Wyoming, where her mother grew up, and wondered if we could establish some type of business there. I suggested looking for a motel, because we could probably live on the premises while taking care of the maintenance and laundry ourselves. My father, besides his main job, had owned a couple of different businesses, so I was comfortable with the idea of owning and running one myself. Tammy was troubled with the risk at first, but as the stress with J.T. began to mount, she began to agree that running a motel might be a solution.

In late 1990 or early 1991, we subscribed to the Sunday edition of the *Billings Gazette* out of Billings, Montana and watched for classified listings of motels that we might be able to afford. We soon discovered that these were few and far between. Our search began before the Internet was widely available, so we had to use old-fashioned methods to obtain information. Tammy had informed her family in Wyoming and Montana that we were looking for a turnkey business. We soon heard about two motels for sale around her mother's hometown. Tammy took a trip with J.T. to look at both locations. We made an offer on one of them, but the owners didn't accept it because the down payment was too low.

We had one more property to view. There were some questions about the finances for this particular motel, which meant we weren't too excited about it, but we went ahead and made an offer on it anyway. The owner's husband was ill, which made her a motivated seller, so she was eager to work with us on the down payment and willing to finance it herself. With the former owners holding the mortgage, we found ourselves the owner/managers of a fourteen-room motel in the small town of Greybull, Wyoming.

We planned to take possession of the motel near the end of June. Now we would both be home to take care of J.T., not just the parent who wasn't working. Since we both wanted to be involved in his life, the move seemed like the right thing to do, but we definitely worried about our financial security on the drive to Greybull. We had sold one of our pickup trucks, cashed out all of our savings and Tam had also borrowed money from her father and grandfather, and we still barely had the down payment.

The finality of the situation hit us as we packed the last item into the rented U-Haul and our remaining vehicle and began our trip to Wyoming. Besides scrimping to come up with a down payment, I had just quit a lucrative programming job in San Diego and Wyoming seemed so far away from the big city where we had made our home for several years. In the end, though, the move would allow us to spend more time with J.T., which we all liked very much. That is what this whole migration revolved around: togetherness.

The motel brought in about $50,000 a year, from which we had to pay the maid, the motel mortgage and the loan from Tam's father and grandfather. If we had been able to do all of the work ourselves, we could have saved the salary for the maid. But J.T. needed more of our attention, so we needed the help. Then we were free to blow anything extra on luxuries like food, heat, etc. Before all of this had even transpired, we put in quite a lot of effort closing the motel deal, during which time we fielded some good questions from our families. How would we survive on so little income? Were we really sure we could squeak by in this new venture? How would we supplement our income if we had to? I figured that I could always find a part-time software job if the need arose.

After a very long drive, and with a very active toddler and a dog in tow, we finally made it to Wyoming. The day before we moved into the motel, Tam's grandfather found a high school student in need of some cash. He helped us unload the U-Haul and move a refrigerator from her grandmother's house. We offloaded most of the boxes into the front room of our living quarters and set up the beds. The small front office was right next to the living room, which made for a very short commute to work.

We finally took possession at the end of June of 1991 and, to our pleasant surprise, the place filled with guests on our very first night as the new owners. Tam and I were ecstatic. At least we wouldn't go broke right away. We had moved all of the boxes into the house, but since we were busy every day cleaning rooms and checking in guests, we were just too tired to unpack the boxes in our front room until the tourist season was over. We lived out of those boxes for a few months while we worked and took care of J.T., who was now a year-and-a-half old. At least the beds had been unpacked and assembled, so we did have something to collapse onto at night.

The work was exhausting and we were dead-tired every night. The morning after our first shift, we watched as our housekeeper, an older lady, flew past us to clean the rooms. This woman was 20 years older than me, yet she raced ahead of me and finished eight rooms, plus made beds in several of the six rooms I managed to clean. All of the rooms were cleaned and ready to rent out by noon, but Tam still had to do the laundry. We ate a quick lunch – something from the A&W restaurant behind us, I think – and collapsed for a short nap before finishing the laundry.

Our siesta lasted but two hours. We arose groggy and sore, and faced a mountain of laundry that needed folding and storing. Meanwhile, J.T. was just getting started. He ran everywhere and checked out everything, the front yard of the motel, our back yard and the entire house. Tam finished the laundry at around six that evening, and we manned the front desk and started the whole process again. I think we filled up early that day as well, but everything from that summer is a blur because of how much we had to do and how exhausted we were at the end of every day before we got into shape.

During that first summer, there was no time to worry about finances, because we worked from sunup to sundown. Sometimes I would have to get up in the middle of the night to address a guest's concerns. Fortunately for our health and sanity, things slowed down in the fall as schools re-opened and tourist traffic began to slow. After that little breather, we decided to close the motel for the season due to low traffic. There was one final bump in traffic for October's hunting season, the highway slowed to a crawl as winter settled into the state.

We had had a good summer season and were overjoyed to put up the sign in late October: CLOSED. That winter, Tam and I finally unpacked the rest of the boxes in the front room and put everything away. We spent the rest of the winter deep-cleaning the motel rooms and preparing for next season.

The first winter was warmer than usual, so we spent lots of time outside. We were raking leaves in February of that year while J.T. wore a light coat while swinging in the swing set out front. Tam and I both worked on cleaning the motel rooms to get them ready for the spring inspection by AAA. However, we had from November until April to clean and we enjoyed the break from our hectic schedule. I believe we even took a weekend to go to a cabin in the mountains by Yellowstone National Park. J.T. seemed to enjoy having both of us around and the winter break was a nice respite from the stress we had dealt with in San Diego. Even though J.T. was behind in his speech, he interacted with us and there was no autism diagnosis at that time. That winter was probably our best time as a family while we lived in Wyoming.

We owned that motel for several years and during that time, several things happened that were a bit out of the ordinary. You get to learn a lot about people when you run a motel. These experiences don't have much to do with autism, but they were a part of our life and allowed us to see the differences in other families. Almost everyone falls under the wide area of a bell curve–that portion I would consider normal people. Then you have the wackos. First, a nice young couple checked in for their honeymoon. After about thirty minutes, another car with a group of people pulled up and wanted us to give them a key to the very same room so they could sneak in and surprise the newlyweds while they were consummating their relationship. I told them no. They persisted, yet I again very firmly denied their request. They finally drove off, looking very disappointed that they weren't able to "surprise" the couple.

Another poor honeymoon couple had some friends who came in to pay for the room. They wanted to put rice in the bed and Vaseline on the toilet seat as a prank. They changed their minds about the toilet when I told them we would charge extra for any damage to the rooms. It turns out that we dodged a bullet—another motel in town had to clean their carpets after pranksters had sprayed whipped cream and shaving cream all over another honeymoon couple's hotel room.

All these different incidents and personalities gave us additional problems to deal with besides our son's autism. We soon discovered that constantly cleaning other people's messes is not as fun as it sounds. We manned the front desk from six to midnight—and sometimes later—checking guests into their rooms. Then we would have to get up at the crack of dawn to check people out of their rooms and begin the cleaning process. The tourist season was so busy that people would stay anywhere. Sometimes, when no motels in the area had any vacancies, people paid to park their cars in our lot and sleep in the vehicles. This gave them the use of the ice machine and the phone in the office. One night, five people took the only room we had left. It was the smallest in the place. They could barely fit inside standing up, but somehow they managed.

Then came the guests with other issues. One man checked in looking sober as a judge, but in reality he was quite drunk. When he left, I discovered that he had vomited all over the room. We had the maid clean the place, but we threw away the linens. There was also the man who tried to flush a glass down the toilet. Little things like that tended to spice up our tenure at the motel, but after five years of cleaning up after people, Tam and I agreed that we wouldn't manage a property again—not even rentals.

In the meantime, J.T. was growing up and busying himself by exploring the place while we took care of things. By then, most of the townspeople either knew us or had heard about us. They enjoyed driving by while J.T. ran around in his shorts and brandished the water hose. That was one thing he enjoyed immensely at that age. He watered everything—including himself. He was constantly grabbing the hose and drowning the front lawn.

At around two years old, he started using a computer. He learned the alphabet using software with cartoon characters. We did have to protect the computer switch, though. He was absolutely delighted at our reactions when he unplugged the computer while we were busy working on it. He also began lengthy temper tantrums on a daily basis around the age of two. During these outbursts, he was inconsolable for almost a half-hour and would fight any efforts to comfort him. These tantrums occurred at least once a day and continued for nearly two years. I think incidents like this are now called "meltdowns." At that time, Tam and I didn't have a clue as to what was wrong or how to fix it. We eventually learned to just be there for him and wait until he calmed himself. Sometimes we would actually sit with him until he went to sleep after he had concluded his screaming, crying and thrashing fit.

However, he still didn't talk as much as other children his age. At best, he said one or two words at a time, but he wouldn't put any sentences together. He also seemed to have problems understanding commands of more than two or three words. Even short directions sometimes had to be repeated before he would pay attention. Since he wouldn't always respond when people spoke to him, someone mentioned that he might be deaf. These people, just as my mother before them, had not been there as he came running when Tam or I opened the front door as quietly as we could in a vain attempt to sneak out of the house. Although we didn't talk about it at the time, Tam and I had begun to believe that something was wrong with J.T. and that he wasn't just slow. However, based on what we knew at the time, speech milestones were reached between the ages of 12 to 24 months. This meant he was still within a somewhat normal functional range, so we decided to give things time.

During this time, we did see J.T. playing with his toys. He was the only grandson on both sides of the family and the first great-grandchild on Tam's side. It had been several years since there was a young child in either family, which meant that he received lots of clothes and toys. Since we experienced challenges with our finances after this move, the gifts were appreciated and J.T. certainly didn't mind having so many toys to choose from. He enjoyed his toy cars and wooden railroad set, and loved watching cartoon videos. He also liked to organize things into patterns. He would coordinate his toys and other things that he found into patterns laid across the living room floor. He once took my wallet and emptied it onto the floor. Credit cards, photos, business cards—everything was neatly arranged and categorized in rows next to his railroad and car setup.

He also recognized trademarks—some from quite a distance. His vision was very good. I believe it was probably better than 20/20. While we were all on a walk one day, he shouted "Ford!" and pointed directly ahead of us. We looked in that direction and then at each other to try to figure out what had caught his attention. We walked for what seemed another quarter-mile and noticed an old parked car with a Ford logo on the front. We finally realized what he had seen. After that, when he would say anything and point, we knew that there was something ahead that was just too far away for us to see until we got closer.

He also liked to play with the telephone during that phase of his life. He had seen us using it, so he would pick up the receiver and pretend to talk to someone by punching numbers on the handset and uttering gibberish into it. We could make out when he said "hello," but everything else simply didn't make sense. We were glad that he was trying to talk, yet we also wondered if he would ever say anything coherent.

Fortunately, our motel phone wouldn't dial out unless a line was first selected. During the summer, our phone bill was higher, due to guests making long distance calls from the rooms. We looked forward to a lower phone bill when we were closed. However, we were very surprised when the business received a $900 phone bill! We wondered if J.T. had figured a way to dial out to Japan, or somewhere more exotic and expensive. But since we had decided to close the motel during the off-season, we were reasonably certain that the bill was inaccurate.

After a few months and a complaint to the Wyoming Public Service Commission, we finally got the phone company to admit that they might have made a mistake. The original bill had been based on approximately 10,000 local phone calls made during the 25-day billing period from a 14-room motel with only two phone lines out. This meant that 400 calls had to be placed from our motel every day during the month to numbers that were local, not long distance. However, only 5,000 people lived in the local area. This was not 5,000 households, this was 5,000 people, which included every man, woman and child in a 30-mile radius. This meant that someone would have had to make about 400 calls a day, every day, for those 25 days in order to make 10,000 phone calls. If that person only spent one minute on each phone call, it could have been done on one line in six hours and forty-five minutes each day, but we would have seen the activity on the front-office phone. It would have lit up when the lines were active, and Tam or I would have noticed the light staying on continuously, day after day, if the phone calls had been made. Even J.T. didn't spend that much time playing with the phone, so once we knew the calls billed were local calls, we knew something was off. Eventually, after the Wyoming Public Service Commission called the phone company, the phone company quickly called us back and admitted that their field rep had "read the meter wrong." Once we figured out that J.T. hadn't run up a massive phone bill, we didn't discourage him from playing with it.

Tam tried reading to him, but he wouldn't sit still. He always seemed to focus on something else at story time. He might sit there for a few seconds and stare off into space, but soon he'd just jump up and he was off to the races. He also didn't interact with people the way most children do. One particular Christmas, the local supermarket held a contest with a giant, toy-filled Christmas stocking as the prize. The thing was huge – nearly four feet tall if I remember correctly. Tam entered J.T. into the contest and he won. One of the store managers dropped by our motel later to give it to him, so we brought J.T. to get the stocking and acknowledge that he'd won it. He was around two and he would usually interact with family. However, he took one look at the stocking and dragged it off, like a lion might retrieve its kill. He never even looked at the lady who gave it to him. He just quickly made his way out of the room without so much as an ounce of gratitude or even a glance to any of us. The lady looked a little surprised, so we laughed it off and thanked her. But it seemed odd to us. Toddlers are basically selfish in nature, but most of them will at least look at the person who gave them their gift and try to interact when they get something, but not J.T.

Even though he wouldn't sit still while Tam read to him, at other times he would pick up a book and pretend to read. As he flipped through the pages, he spoke unintelligibly, as if actually telling the story. Tam's mom told us that Tam had done the same thing when she was a toddler. Since Tam interacted with people like other adults, we thought it was another sign that J.T. would grow out of his behavior and eventually start talking more.

He also staged events as he played with his toys. We saw how he mimicked as he arranged the cars and figurines, so we knew he was being creative. But his language did not develop beyond one- or two-word sentences. We thought he might just be what is termed a "late talker." It wasn't until later that we realized the other differences in his behavior.

Tamara

Many years have passed since John-John was a toddler, but I still remember different incidents from that time. My husband and I busied ourselves with the motel during the summer months, but the rest of the year gave us more time as a family. John-John was quite a handful and my depression often caused me to lose patience with him. In addition, his daily tantrums took their toll on us as we tried to deal with his issues. It was frustrating to try to talk to him and know that unless I kept the language very simple, he would not understand anything I said. Yet he played with his toys as if he showed an understanding of the world around him. I just couldn't figure out why he didn't understand what I was saying, even after I repeated it many times over many days. Sometimes, even when I kept things simple, he did not react to me or show that he understood what I had said.

I remember being outside with him during that first summer while I hung sheets on the clothes-line. I would talk to him and try to get his attention, but he was totally focused on playing in the dirt with his toys. In an effort to get him to turn and look at me, I would repeat his name over and over. "John ... John ... John ... John ..." After repeating his name several times, I finally got him to glance over at me, but he would always quickly look back at the dirt and his toys. I gradually repeated his name closer together, which gave rise to his nickname, John-John.

He interacted with the world in other ways and showed capabilities that seemed advanced for his age. I remember one instance when we visited my grandparents. My grandfather had an electric typewriter he used to write to family and friends. John-John was around two when he discovered the typewriter. He had never seen one before—only a printer hooked up to a computer. My grandfather didn't use it when we visited and I never used it either, so as far as I knew John-John had never before seen how one worked. He took one look at that machine and something just clicked. He found a sheet of paper, rolled it into the platen cylinder and started pecking away. These little impromptu acts told us someone was inside that little body and thinking clearly. He simply wasn't very interested in using words to communicate—or maybe he just wasn't able.

In another incident, his behavior showed that he seemed behind in his basic comprehension skills. I had been busy taking care of items for the motel rooms when I came into the house to check on John-John. Imagine my surprise when I walked into our living room to find that he decided to flood the area with water from the hose just outside the back door. I remember walking in and seeing John-John standing there, holding the hose and aiming it toward the middle of the living room. A quarter-inch of water was seeping from behind him and the back porch, which he had already drenched. After I got over my initial shock and after several sloshing steps through the water, I blew up. John-John had a big smile on his face as he pointed the hose into the living room, but when he saw me, he grew serious, dropped the hose and ran off toward the back yard. I knew that I was too angry to go after him, so I shut off the water, got some towels and started mopping up what I could. When I yelled for John, he came in and helped me clean up the mess. The carpet was still soggy, so we ended up borrowing a carpet cleaner from my grandmother. We used that to soak up the water and empty it outside. It took us an hour or so, but we finally dried the carpet.

After the clean-up – and after I cooled off – I found John-John, brought him to the back door where the hose was stored and said "NO!" while pointing to the hose, then pointing back to the living room where the carpet had been flooded. I repeated this several times and when he tried to run off, I would pick him up, point toward the hose, then toward the living room and repeat "no" and "no water." He fussed and cried for a bit, then I let him go and he ran away from the hose and the living room to his play area in the yard. I felt satisfied that I had done my parental duty and that he probably wouldn't repeat the act, at least for a while. I knew he was a child and that, as a parent, you had to repeat lessons several times before a child learned from the instruction. I also had experience that if an adult was firm enough with a child, they would usually not do something naughty for a few days after they had been scolded.

I initially believed I had gotten the point across about not running the hose in the house, but I found out how wrong I was. A few days later, I walked into the living room and found J.T. with the hose yet again. This time, at least he hadn't flooded as much of the place before I found him. I yelled again, even angrier this time, and he ran off toward the back yard. John and I again cleaned up the mess, but this time I could see that my scolding hadn't worked, so I disconnected the hose and put it away so he couldn't flood our living room again – at least with the hose. I put the hose in the garage and John or I would get it out when we needed to water something out back. I also repeated the phrase "no hose" to John-John over and over again, though I could not tell if he understood or was even paying attention to me. I don't remember him flooding the living room again, so it must have worked. I will offer up what I call a "life pro tip" for other parents of autistic children: I recommend investing in a wet-dry shop vacuum. They are very useful for cleaning up messes like soaked carpets and LEGO bricks – when you've had enough of them – as well as other items.

Hiding or locking up items became a common theme in our family, since John-John either did not understand or forgot about things that he should not do. Given his creativity, I would not have been surprised if he brought buckets to the kitchen sink, filled them up and dragged them into the living room to create his next masterpiece. It almost seemed as if he felt that this was something he needed to do.

When I look over his early pictures, I am reminded of another difference with our family. I have many images I took of him with my 35mm camera. I also have professional shots of him at six months, one-

and–a-half years and two-and–a-half years. However, I don't have school pictures of him or professional pictures after he turned two. Most children have their pictures taken at school each year, but because we homeschooled him, we didn't have those pictures. The last picture taken by a professional was a family picture, and it was then that I became impressed with family photographers.

I had talked John into going with us so that we could have a family picture taken. We went to a local department store and had to wait for 30 minutes while another family had their pictures taken. In the meantime, John-John was getting upset about waiting for so long and John was getting frustrated because John-John was upset. By the time it was our turn, my husband and son were both tired and ready to leave. I was unhappy because I figured that our pictures were going to show a surly husband and a screaming child. I was not disappointed. John-John did cry during most of the photos and John and I were muttering under our breath, wondering if the photographer was ever going to take a picture or keep posing us. John vowed to never have a family photo taken again and I decided I would not go to a photographer anytime soon. However, when we saw our pictures, we looked like a normal, happy family. There were smiles on my face and John's, and John-John appearing to be laughing in one shot. I looked closer at the images in later years and I realized that the photographer timed the shots so that my screaming child instead looked like he was opening his mouth in laughter. He also caught John and me grimacing so that it also looked like we were smiling. The photographer certainly earned his pay that day. I had ordered plenty of copies since I knew that it was unlikely that we would ever have a family portrait again.

During all of these events, I felt a little uneasy, as if something was off with John-John, but his behaviors were still in line with milestones for other toddlers, based on the criteria at the time, so I ignored those feelings. As a teenager, I had helped take care of my sister and I had watched over toddlers, so I knew that children didn't always follow commands. But with J.T. it was different. He didn't seem to care about consequences or react to any of our reprimands, even when we became very upset with him as he experimented with projects like soaking the carpet. He would just run off – humming as he went – and appearing to not care about our speaking or yelling at him. He would run to and fro, inside the house in cold weather or outside when it was warmer. He just sprinted back and forth, humming the entire time. Sometimes I would try to talk to him as he did this, but he would appear to ignore me and eventually I gave up. His running and humming simply became a background behavior that he performed in between his other activities.

I now realize that he was "stimming," a form of self-stimulation as a way to reduce his anxiety. While this is associated with autism, nearly everyone stims. It's just that some forms are more acceptable than others. For example, many people drum their fingers or tap a foot when they are anxious or don't like their current situation. With autistic people, their stimming tends to be more noticeable and is frowned upon as childish behavior, or as an annoyance due to the noise and energy exhibited. Though this is widely known now thanks to the existence of autistic support groups and communities, this was essentially unknown when John-John was young, and it had become just one more frustrating behavior pattern to deal with.

Another aspect of his conduct that is quite frustrating to this day is inappropriate giggling. For example, when he would get something he wasn't supposed to play with, I would yell at him to stop. He would drop the item, giggle, and run off. Or he would play roughly with the dog and when she would snap at him, he would giggle at her behavior. While researching for this book, I remembered times when I giggled inappropriately while I was growing up and it suddenly dawned on me that his giggles were not from amusement, but instead due to nervousness. Unfortunately, when he was younger and he giggled after I found another of his messes, I didn't always remain calm, because I thought he was trying to be funny. Now I can see that he was probably nervous because of the situation and he giggled as a result. This is one of those things that, if I had learned about it sooner, it would have made it easier to work with his behavior and try to reduce his anxiety instead of increasing it by yelling at him.

Another phenomenon I noticed concerning John-John's condition occurred when he began his "terrible twos." I had read how children at that age would say "no" to everything an adult might ask, even if it was something they actually wanted. I thought about this and figured that the reason children might say no all the time is that the behavior had been modeled for them. With toddlers, who are very busy exploring their world, parents will say no quite often to their children. I thought that children repeat what they have been taught and if they have only heard "no" in a firm tone, they will repeat it as a way to try to gain control over the world around them. I reasoned that children might have simply repeated mannerisms they had seen and just needed a different behavior model.

When John-John started crawling and reaching for things, instead of saying "no" all the time, I would say "thank you" when I took something from him that he wasn't supposed to have. This worked until he was around two-and-a-half. I still remember the day I sat holding something when he ran up to me, grabbed it right out of my hands and said "thank you!" and he ran off with it. I was so surprised that I didn't react for nearly a minute. Then it hit me: He had learned that it was okay to grab things out of people's hands, so long as he said "thank you" after he did it. I had a good laugh at myself and decided that I once again must alter my approach in teaching him proper manners.

I now realize that it also shows his literal approach to learning the language at that time. Later in his development, he also had problems with the pronoun usages of "I," "me" and "you." He would use "you" when he was talking about himself and "me" or "I" when referring to others. To John-John, he was "you" because that is how he was talked about, while other people were "I" because that was how they referred to themselves. I must admit to having some confusion myself if I think too much about it. I'm amazed that anybody figures out how to change the context of those two words.

Since John and I were busy running the motel, we shrugged off our worries and figured he was just slow to talk. My mother shared that I had been slow to talk as well, and also had been thought of as "behind the curve." In talking with my mom and dad when I was older, I told them that I had memories from right before my third birthday and that I didn't say much to other people because I didn't have anything to talk about. Based on my memories, my mom's stories and seeing John-John's interaction with his environment, I figured he would eventually catch up. I found myself wishing that this would happen sooner rather than later, so that he and I would not become frustrated in communicating with each other.

Resources, References, and Reflections — Signs of Autism in Toddlers

Looking back at John-John's toddler years, I remember feeling uneasy about some of his behaviors, but pushing back my worries and figuring that I was just an over-protective first-time mother and that my son was probably normal. I can also see that it was easy to interpret his acts as bad behavior, when it was more likely that most of it was caused by his difficulties in communicating and understanding the rules of the normal world. The move to Wyoming removed many stresses on our family, but I was still concerned about appearing normal and having my child behave. Based on what I have learned in the last year, I wish I had known that some of his behaviors were probably the result of his inability to understand us and his attempt to make sense of the world. I also think there was and is a mischievous side to my son, and that some behaviors were just him acting out to test the limits of what he could and could not do. The problem is to try to figure out which behavior is which, so that firmness and understanding are used in the right combination. Too much firmness can lead to anxiety and uncertainty in the child, but too much understanding can lead to inappropriate behavior. It is a difficult balancing act for any parent and more so for a parent of an autistic child, due to the communication issues.

I can also see that there were signs of my son's problems long before we heard a diagnosis of autism. In most cases, I think parents should trust their gut instincts about their child. They are around their child most of the time and professionals sometimes downplay parents' concerns as over-protectiveness. While there are parents who do not have the right skills or who need help in parenting, I believe that many parents should trust themselves more and look at what is right for their family, not what is considered right for the average family – or worse, what's easier for the professional to deal with. Early intervention can help autistic children learn to interact with the world sooner and it can be important to get the additional help that might make a difference for that child. However, I also believe that children continue to change, so that even if some of the early opportunities are missed, the child will not stop completely in their development.

For parents who are feeling a bit uneasy or unsure, autism research has revealed that early intervention can help in reaching children on the spectrum. A checklist of behaviors was created in order to help find possible autism at earlier ages than in the past. A study has shown that the use of a checklist at 18 months or younger can identify autism or other developmental delays.[2] When John-John was a toddler, diagnosis usually didn't occur until a child was three or older. Now it takes place at two years of age or younger. This early diagnosis can be used to increase interaction with the child and improve their ability to communicate verbally. However, in some cases, there are physical issues with verbal communication, so other methods of communication should be explored with the child. It is likely that the child is trying to communicate with the parents, but it may be subtle and non-verbal, and very difficult to detect. With computers and various other media,

---

[2] *Validation of the Infant-Toddler Checklist as a Broadband Screener for Autism Spectrum Disorders from 9 to 24 Months of Age*, Amy M. Wetherby, Susan Brosnam-Maddox, Vickie Peace and Laura Newton, *Autism,* September 2008
http://www.ncbi.nlm.nih.gov/pmc/articles/PMC2663025/?tool=pubmed

there are many more options available for working with a child on their communication skills.

"Assessment & Diagnosis" *Autism Research Institute*. N.p., 2016. Web. 24 Mar. 2016.

Fernell, Elisabeth, Mats Anders Eriksson, and Christopher Gillberg. "Early Diagnosis of Autism and Impact on Prognosis: A Narrative Review" *Clinical Epidemiology* 5 (2013): 33–43. *PMC*. Web. 24 Mar. 2016.

"Screening And Diagnosis" *CDC – Facts about Autism Spectrum Disorders – NCBDDD*. N.p., 2015. Web. 24 Mar. 2016.

"What Is Autism? Autism Science Foundation" *Autism Science Foundation*. N.p., 2015. Web. 24 Mar. 2016.

4

Seeing a Problem

John

In spite of the little things we noticed, Tam and I figured that J.T. would catch up with other kids before he reached school age. However, in early 1993, events forced us to look again at his progress. Just before his third birthday, J.T. contracted the stomach flu. This was the first time he had ever been sick, so we figured he would get over it in a couple of days, as most kids do. He couldn't eat or drink much of anything during that week, so we finally took him to the doctor, who diagnosed him with severe dehydration. Tam and I took him to the hospital after that visit and they gave him intravenous fluids. After a night of observation and rehydration, he finally kept his food down and looked much better. After the hospital released him, he made a complete recovery and was quickly back to running around and humming to himself. However, this incident really frightened us. We still get nervous when he comes down with anything, especially a stomach virus.

While J.T. was in the hospital, the doctor and nurses noticed how he reacted to his new surroundings. Once he felt better, he just wouldn't calm down. It was late in the evening and Tammy was exhausted after taking care of him for the past week. Since I usually had the calmer relationship with him, I stayed with him so Tam could go home and get some rest after being up with him for several nights and taking care of him all day. When she left, he was already asleep in bed. As the I.V. did its work, he started feeling better and woke up, but was unhappy about being in the hospital with a needle in the back of his hand. He started one of his tantrums and tried to pull out the needle. Two nurses and I tried to calm him down, but he wouldn't respond to us. I frantically called home and asked Tammy to come back to the hospital. It certainly was a long twenty minutes while I waited for her, but once she walked into the room, he immediately calmed down and stopped his outburst. It surprised both of us, because while he would interact with Tam, I was the one he usually turned to for comfort. She ended up staying the night to keep him calm. Due to Tammy's depression, she had her own problems in dealing with J.T. and I usually provided a more stable parental figure for him.

The nurses noticed this right away. We heard a rumor a few weeks later that one of them wondered if he was abused because of what they saw during his hospital stay. They didn't feel that Tammy reacted properly to how poorly he was coming along and that he acted like a starved child. They also didn't think well of her for leaving him with me and having to be called back to the hospital. He hadn't eaten for a week, so he was quite thin, and since we were really exhausted from taking care of a very sick child while running a motel at the same time, we didn't have a lot of energy left to react to his situation. Fortunately, when hospital staffers talked to people who knew us, they learned how wrong they were, so we never saw anyone from Child Services. But the rumors really worried us.

During the follow-up visit, the doctor mentioned that J.T. should probably have been speaking more by this age and that a pre-school in the next town worked with children who experienced developmental delays. We decided to check it out, so we visited the school and talked to a teacher who gave us a tour of the facility. We even asked about a play group for him, because we thought it might be a good first step in his development, but the only group they had was already full. Instead, she recommended that he attend a few sessions at the pre-school so they could assess him.

We agreed, as long as Tammy could come with him and sit in on the session. We kept this schedule once or twice a week for almost a month, all the while asking for their thoughts about J.T., but only getting vague answers from the faculty. After a few weeks, the school sent home a booklet about an IEP, or individualized education program. It outlined how a school could develop a plan to help children with learning disabilities. This seemed like a good idea, until we came to the line that described how the state could enforce compliance. We had heard stories about CPS coming into homes and taking children away from parents and we were concerned that the school might call to take J.T. into foster care so that he would have to attend the school whether we agreed or not. We had read horror stories about Child Services, about the vengeful neighbors who called them, and parents and their children being separated based on little or no proof, or negative interpretations of treatment of the children[1]. We felt strongly that J.T. was better off with us because of the stories about CPS at that time.

---

[1] In the early '90s, newspaper articles focused attention on the abuses of CPS when investigating families. Since that time, court cases have affirmed the rights of parents, but by 1993, case law had not yet been established. Examples of CPS overreach in the '90s are *Calabretta v. Floyd* and another case in Escondido, California (Wallis v. Spencer - https://isc.idaho.gov/cp/caselaw/fed/Wallis%20v.%20Spencer%20202%20F.3d%2011 26.pdf). In the *Calabretta v. Floyd* case, CPS came to a house with a police officer and no warning because of an anonymous tip of child abuse. The children were strip-searched, but no evidence of abuse was found and no further action was taken. The parents sued and the court ruled that unless there is an emergency, a warrant is required and CPS cannot force their way into a home. The incident occurred in 1995. http://caselaw.findlaw.com/us-9th-circuit/1149036.html

In the Escondido, CA case, CPS seized two children based on a tip from a family member. The children were seized in the middle of the night with the aid of the police. No evidence of abuse was found, but the children were kept in foster care for two and half months. When the children were returned, the family was billed for foster care. In this case the justices ruled that authorities must get family consent or a judge's order before an invasive examination of a minor. This case occurred in September 1999. http://californiahomeschool.net/howTo/cps.htm

After Tam's observations at the pre-school and our own fears about CPS being called in, we were very concerned about J.T.'s possible status in public school. Because of our fear of CPS and our lack of knowledge of our rights, our immediate concern was that the state would try to take our son from us. The IEP further stipulated that the state couldn't act before the plan was finalized, so we pulled him out of that school and never brought him back. We wanted to take action before the state took over.

Suddenly the school was ready to talk to us. They told us how concerned they were about J.T. and how they felt it was not wise of us to remove him from the curriculum. We asked them why they hadn't talked to us before we withdrew J.T. from school, and why we never got a good answer when we did ask questions. We felt like they had left us out of the loop, while at the same time it seemed like they thought we should let the school handle everything.

After what Tammy had witnessed in J.T.'s pre-school, we decided that it was best to keep him away from that institution and see what we could do on our own. We felt better about our decision later when we talked to a teacher at one of the public schools. We found out that the pre-school didn't have a good reputation for how it handled children and parents. We might have enrolled him in another pre-school, but there were no others in the immediate area. There were probably others in towns farther away, but that would have meant driving an hour or more one way, and during winter that could have been dangerous. For parents in larger towns with more choices, there are many options for schools that are more compatible, but in our case we didn't feel that we had that flexibility.

In spite of our experience at the pre-school, Tammy and I realized that there was more going on with J.T. than just his language skills. While he interacted with people, he would also go off into his own little world. He experienced problems with understanding sentences longer than a few words and we had already noticed he did not answer to his own name unless we repeated it.

We had also heard of a condition that had been occurring with more and more children. Someone had named it "autism." The first time either of us even heard the term was when we saw the movie *Rain Man*, but we didn't want to believe J.T. was like that. The only other information we had suggested institutionalizing children, because only professionals knew how to handle them. I knew that was not the right future for him and Tammy agreed. We knew that J.T. was an intelligent person. At this point, we began trying to figure out how to reach the bright boy we knew him to be.

Tamara

The year John-John turned three was very stressful for us. It began with his illness and I remember feeling helpless as we tried to help him recover. It was made harder that week as we experienced extremely cold weather, with highs below freezing, even during the day. I was quite familiar with the stomach flu. I had often had it myself, so I didn't think much of it when John-John first started throwing up. I figured he would be sick for a day or so and then get better. He did vomit less after the first day, but he never stopped completely and couldn't keep anything down. I tried to give him liquids, but he either didn't want them or didn't keep them down very long. His illness began on a Monday, and my worries increased as the week progressed. I wasn't aware of dehydration in a young child and I wasn't thinking very clearly, due to my lack of sleep while caring for him. Part of me looked for any signs of progress, but I also worried that he probably wasn't getting enough to eat or drink. The house was very cold and the fireplace didn't warm the place as much as it could. John-John and I would stay in the living room at night to keep warm, and I experienced very fitful sleep as he got up periodically to wander around or throw up again.

By the end of the week, John and I were both very worried and finally decided that we needed to take him to the doctor. We took John-John in for an office visit and the doctor looked him over. We were told that our son needed to go to the hospital, so we had him checked there. His kidney function was low, so they recommended we check him overnight and have an IV inserted. John and I agreed and we checked him in. He was very sick, he laid in the hospital bed and didn't even react when they inserted the needle into his hand. I stayed for a short time, but I was exhausted from the strain of the week. John said he would stay and we both figured that John-John would stay calmer with him there. I drove home and dropped into bed, falling asleep as soon as I laid down.

I awoke sometime later, very groggy, to the phone ringing. I made my way to the front office. John told me that I needed to come back to try and calm John-John down. I could hear him crying in the background and my heart sank at the news. If John couldn't calm him, then he must be very upset and I worried that something else was wrong. I dressed, locked up and took off for the hospital. It was bitter cold but the roads were clear, so I didn't have to worry about ice or snow on my drive. When I arrived at the hospital, I ran to the door, only to be stopped by a sign that read "Ring for entrance." I rang the bell, but no one answered. I rang the bell again, but still nothing. I became frustrated because I was only a few feet away from my son and husband, but could not help them. I finally thought to open the door. Surprised it was open after hours, I went in and noticed the front desk was empty. When I got to our son's room, I realized that the two nurses on duty were trying to calm my son and keep him from pulling out his I.V. When he saw me, he put his arms out and I went to hold him. He still cried, but he calmed down and quit trying to pull his IV out. Since I had some sleep before coming back, I was able to stay the rest of the night.

In the morning, I was happy to see my son doing better. He wanted the IV out, but he remained quiet while we talked to the staff. They ran some tests and agreed to remove the IV. They also agreed that we could take him home, since he was doing well. He was finally able to keep his food down and after the five days of throwing up, this was a wonderful thing. I was still tired, but when we got home, we were even more surprised to find out that my aunt and grandmother had come over to set up a buffet for John-John so he could eat. He was a little hesitant at first, but he eventually went over and started sampling all of the food to make up for lost time. I was still somewhat nervous about him keeping all that food down, but after a few hours with nothing happening, I felt relieved. I don't remember much about that night, except that we all slept very soundly after a very stressful week.

When we later heard that the staff had accused us of abusing him, it was a blow to our family and an indication that something was off. I can see now that my own insecurities didn't help matters, either. I had wanted to delay going to the doctor because I was so uncomfortable around them and I was worried about what they might do or say. I am glad we did finally act, but even this experience didn't change my lack of trust. I felt like something needed to be done to help John-John, but with the rumors of child abuse being passed around, my trust in institutions was lowered. I had no idea what to do and yet I had little hope of professional help. I felt comfortable with the doctor who had seen John-John, so we went back for a follow-up and asked for suggestions. He mentioned the pre-school and once again mentioned his concerns about John-John's speech. I didn't like the idea of seeking outside help, but I also felt very lost. So after I talked with John, we decided to see if the pre-school could help.

When I first heard of the pre-school, I felt it might help. I remember when I attended pre-school. It was a time without negative memories about social situations. I figured that pre-school could be a place where John-John could be around other children and still be himself. I would have preferred a playgroup, but because of my issues with social interaction, I had no idea how to find one in our small town. Many of the social interactions occurred because of church or school, and since we were not involved with either, I had not met very many people. My grandparents knew some people, but they were older and didn't have young children. If someone initiated a social interaction with me, I could hold my own, but I had no idea how to meet other people.

John and I had agreed that pre-school might be the answer, but because of my mistrust with institutions and John-John's inability to talk about his experiences, I asked to sit in on John-John's classes. The teacher agreed, so twice a week for the next month or so, I observed while our son participated in his activities. Some elements of his new surroundings seemed helpful during this time. John-John enjoyed getting out, but he did not play with the other children. Instead, he would play with toys and participate in some of the activities. He had problems with some elements of the educational experience, and other incidents that did not seem helpful troubled me as well. Because of my trust issues, I decided to keep quiet and see if things would improve.

Before John-John attended the school, a teacher gave me a tour of the facility. We saw the various play areas and she described the children's activities. I liked what I saw and there didn't seem to be too much focus on things like reading or sitting still. At one point, the teacher showed me a wall of art from the students and said, "We are proud of our pre-school. We feel it will prepare the children well for school." This did not sit well with me and I felt myself becoming angry. I wanted my child to be ready to live his life, not just get by in school. I understand that school can be important, but I also know that there is a lot more to the world than a classroom. Part of this attitude comes from my experiences in grade school and high school, where I was teased and bullied due to my differences. I didn't say anything to his teacher, though, because I knew I was biased and I only wanted to help my child. In spite of my mistrust toward the school system, I knew that I needed to give things a fair chance, since it might help my son. I started taking John-John to class and I would sit in a corner while he interacted with the other children and the teachers. I realized that he might not have the same experience I did and I needed to put aside my feelings to see if this new environment would be good for him.

I observed without interacting with John-John or the other children. If he came to me, I would turn him around and point him back to the other children. I don't remember this happening very often after the first time. This pre-school had scheduled unstructured time for the children to play, as well as other times for activities and to learn the alphabet, numbers and manners for behaving around other children. From what I remember, John-John usually played by himself, but would occasionally interact with the other children. During each of our two-hour sessions, the teachers were busy with all of the children. I don't remember all of the details after so many years, but I do recall two incidents that disturbed me.

The first episode occurred during unstructured playtime while the children interacted in ways that modeled real-world events. They had a kitchen, a store counter and a workshop in which to be creative. John-John went to the store area, another child chose the kitchen and a third played in the workshop. A fourth child watched from the side while playing with some loose toys. After a few minutes, the other children moved over to the kitchen area and began playing with each other, while John-John busied himself at the store counter. Presently, he looked up and watched the others for a minute or so, then went to join them.

I was really happy to see him trying to play with the other children. Then the teacher stepped in and told him he couldn't stay in that area. She turned him around and pointed him toward another play station. He looked at her with a puzzled expression, resisted, and then finally went to play by himself. I shook my head as the teacher explained that there was a limit of three children per play station and he needed to learn the rules. I thought the point was for my son to learn how to play with other children, but apparently, I was wrong.

Another incident occurred during snack time. A plate of cookies was passed around and the children had to ask for their treat. John-John didn't understand, but when the teacher told him that he needed to ask, he responded with something that sounded like it included the word "please." Again, I was happy he was responding, but apparently it wasn't clear enough, so the teacher wouldn't give him his cookie. He reached for the snack, but the teacher pulled the plate away, to which he responded with a temper tantrum/meltdown. I stepped in to let her know what I had seen and the teacher reluctantly let him have a cookie, which calmed him down. I did not disagree that children need to learn to speak and be polite, but when difficulties arise, a child's effort should be recognized in order to encourage positive social behavior in the future.

This narrow focus on exact behaviors did not sit well with me. To me, this type of training only recognizes perfect actions and does not take into account the difficulties some children might experience in performing very basic tasks that their peers can easily accomplish. If a child never receives recognition of effort based on what they can and cannot do, they can become discouraged. In addition, I observed the interactions of the teachers with other children that continued focusing on rules for rules' sake. I have experience with children acting up and testing adults, but I also recognize that sometimes children don't know everything and sometimes they need guidance instead of punishment. Based on my observations, I felt that there was too much focus on obeying rules, with little or no support and guidance to help children at their own level of development.

These two incidents, along with my other observations, stayed with me. They focused on the rules and the children all had to follow them to the letter, no matter their skill level. The base assumption appeared to be that all children had the exact same abilities, even though pre-school was supposed to target children with different learning abilities and difficulties. I understood that children need to learn rules, but my experience with our son indicated to me that he didn't even know rules existed – or that something kept him from understanding those rules in the same way as other children. Without extra guidance to help him see outside structure, he would be frustrated and punished for something he could not help.

After a month of this situation, I talked with John about what I had observed. I knew that I was biased and John will often help me to see when I might be overreacting to situations that are normal for everyone else. Both of us wanted to help John-John, but after our discussion we felt misgivings about this pre-school and its methods for working with children. After several discussions, we both felt that John-John's development was simply not progressing in pre-school as we would have liked, so we asked for a meeting with the teachers. We went to the school after hours and met with the faculty in a small room. John and I sat on one side of the table and the three teachers sat on the other side. I asked them for their thoughts on what had happened in the classroom, but no one gave a clear answer to any of our questions.

"It's been a few weeks," I began. "Can you tell us what you think might be going on?"

"We still need some more time to evaluate John-John," one of them replied. "We aren't sure of what we are observing."

"Do you have some idea of what's wrong?" I asked. "Can you at least give us an idea of what we might be dealing with? Is it just delayed speech, or are there other problems?"

Another teacher took this set of questions. "We think it's too early to discuss what the problems might be. We'd like a little more time to evaluate him."

We continued to ask questions in an effort to gain some idea of what we might be dealing with, but we always got the same answer: They needed more time for evaluation and weren't ready to tell us what they thought might be wrong. After the meeting, John and I talked it over. Our impression was that we worried too much and maybe the teachers knew the best methods for handling the situation. We still had our misgivings about their methods, but we also felt that something was wrong with John-John. We decided to trust the pre-school.

I continued to go with John-John for another week or so. After one of our visits, and because of our questions and requests for more information, we received a bright yellow booklet that explained our rights and something called an Individualized Education Plan, or IEP. I now understand much more about IEPs, but at the time John and I did not know anything about them or any of our rights. We had heard stories about Child Protective Services (CPS) and how they would take children away from families because of false reports of abuse. We were very sensitive about him being taken away because of his behavior, so this thought was always in the back of our minds. While reading through the booklet, I saw a passage about how the state had the right to step in and do whatever it felt necessary to follow the IEP once the plan had been set up[2].

Since I tended to be quite literal with my interpretations, I was very concerned about John-John being taken from us and became quite worried. I began to question our decision. What if the state took him away from us in order to make sure the plan was followed? Based on what I had observed at the pre-school, I did not feel confident that the

---

[2] A case filed after our pre-school experience is a prime example of schools stepping in to take steps against parental objections. This case concerned the homeschooling of a child with special needs in 2002. Parents had attempted to get help for their child from public schools for several years and finally withdrew their child for homeschooling after numerous failures. The schools then attempted to force an evaluation for services, which the parents did not want. The school district initiated a due-process hearing under the Federal Disabilities in Education Act (IDEA) to force them to have their child evaluated. The parents fought the case and it was eventually ruled that the IDEA law did not give public schools authority over homeschooled children with special needs. Camdenton R-III School District v. Mr. and Mrs. F, http://media.ca8.uscourts.gov/opndir/06/03/043102P.pdf

teachers would avoid this option. I definitely had a gut feeling that they felt they were right and would do whatever they felt necessary to "help" our child.

That pre-school was probably the right choice for many families, but with my misgivings about the teaching methods and the passage about the state stepping in to implement their own plan, alarm bells went off in my head. John and I both had issues with what had been happening. We decided not to enroll John-John. I know that teachers and schools provide services that have helped families with autistic children, but because of my issues and our concern over how our son was being treated, we thought that the school was not a good match for us.

John and I let the school know that we had decided to withdraw John-John. After we notified them, we got a phone call from the head instructor. She tried to explain how worried they were about him and how they were all very concerned about how he would do without them. I remember the conversation quite well.

"Are you sure you want to take John-John out?" the teacher asked. "We are really concerned about him."

"If you're so concerned, why won't you tell us what you think the problem is?" I asked in return. "You didn't act all that concerned when we met with you last week."

"We have seen signs in his behavior that trouble us," she continued, "and we'd like some more time to evaluate him."

"You've had several weeks to evaluate him," I said, "and you wouldn't share any of your information with us. I'm also concerned about the possibility of the state stepping in to force us into a plan we don't want. I just don't think that would be a good idea."

"It wouldn't come to that," she responded, "and we feel that we can help him. Don't take him out. We just need a little more time."

"You should have told us that when we met with you, and now when we do pull him out, it's suddenly urgent that we keep him in the school," I said. "I'm sorry, this isn't working out. I'm just not comfortable with your approach. I don't feel that you are listening to my husband or to me, and I don't want to work with you anymore."

She tried to get me to change my mind, but the more she talked, the more I was convinced that this school was the wrong place for our son. John and I stood by our decision and we did not take John-John back to that school. However, we still had a problem. John-John was behind with his speech and had issues with social behavior. We didn't quite know what to do, but we didn't think that the experts did, either.

For the short term, we found a speech therapist in another town and I took John-John on a weekly basis to visit with her. While she was a caring person, the sessions didn't help him very much. It was a good place for me to talk with a sympathetic person about our efforts to get our son to talk. However, I did learn some exercises to help him and we saw some improvement over the next few months. Even with these visits, his communication skills still lagged and we just couldn't make a good connection with him.

In addition, the stress took a heavy toll on me and I contracted conjunctivitis and an occurrence of temporomandibular joint disorder, or TMJ. The TMJ occurred in my jaw due to how much I was clenching my teeth. I took a bite of something and heard a 'click' as the left side of my jaw popped out. It was very painful and I had to go to the doctor to get a muscle relaxant to fix the problem. As the year progressed, we also had to face the harsh reality that our finances were not getting any better and that we needed an additional income stream for our family. While we did not have an official diagnosis for John-John's behavior, John and I both felt that he might have a condition we had heard about called autism. Because of our financial worries, I began to research the disorder to try to figure out how it applied to John-John and our family, as well as possible treatments – however costly.

During this time, we also noticed behavior that caused problems. We found out that there was a mischievous side to him. Even though John-John was very bright and knew how to play computer games, he had figured out that he could get wonderful reactions from his parents if he turned off the computer while we were using it. He would flip the switch on the computer and run away giggling, and John or I would become very upset when we lost our work.

Typically, it happened like this: John sat at the computer and focused on the screen while debugging his current program.

Meanwhile, John-John walked up to the side of the computer near the switch. Then he turned it off. "AAGGGHHH!" John yelled as he swiveled in his chair to face him. "John-John, don't do that!" All the while, John-John giggled and grinned at his father.

"NO! Don't turn off the switch while I'm using the computer!" John would tell him again. By this time, John had gotten up to chase after John-John, who now ran from the room, still giggling away. When John brought our son back into the room, he showed him the switch and said "NO!" several times while John-John squirmed to get down. He would then put him down, get back on the computer and then repeat the scenario. This also happened while I worked on the computer – several times a day over the next few days. It got to the point where we couldn't use the computer at all while John-John was awake or he would inevitably turn it off, no matter how loudly we yelled at him. I understood that children like to get reactions from their parents, but normal children stop when they realize how upset their parents are. John-John never reached that stopping point – he would just repeat the behavior no matter how upset John or I got with him.

Since this behavior was very frustrating, I did try to discipline him with time-outs and spankings, but neither method had any positive effect on him. Whenever I placed him on a time-out, he would scream uncontrollably and would not stay in his seat. He just would not be held in place. No matter how many times I tried, he would always react by yelling and fighting to get away. I also tried shutting him in his room as a time-out. My mother had used this method with me. I would have to stay in my room until an adult told me it was okay to come out. With John-John, he would not stay in his room and I would have to hold the door shut as he tried to open it. Spanking also had no effect and would cause him to fight even more. Even when we shouted at him, we could not get his attention. He would just run off or fight us when held. He struggled as hard as he could, each and every time I would try to stop him from acting up. After being kicked and smacked around by a strong, healthy, struggling three-year-old, I finally began to think of ways to stop his behavior before it happened. This included changing the environment by removing access to things like the computer switch or not going to stores where he would want items that he couldn't have.

We gradually realized that we had to find ways to soften the effects of his destructive conduct and reduce how much damage control was required. John eventually bolted a metal housing around the computer switch and we hid an electrical power strip where John-John couldn't reach it, and used it to turn the PC off and on. We had originally used childproof locks on our cabinets, but John-John quickly figured out how to bypass these simple items. Gradually, when John-John was not around to see where we had put them, we removed the dangerous chemicals and other items to higher ground for his safety. We eventually reorganized our kitchen, and items that we didn't mind him playing with – such as pots and pans – were stored on lower shelves, while breakable items like glasses were stored in the cupboards. I had long ago given up on keeping my books on their shelf, so up they went while his books were stored in lower reaches. We continued to use this approach in anticipation of future situations where John-John would repeat acts that were destructive or disruptive.

He showed us another example of his mimicking skills as I cut John's hair one time. I was in the middle of the trim when I had to go out and help a customer in one of the rooms. I was only gone for a few minutes, but when I came back, I found a couple of shaved spots on the back of my husband's head.

"John," I remember asking, "was John-John in here?"

"I think so," he replied. "I think he ran in to get something."

"Did he come in behind you?" I asked as I looked at the bald patches, torn between annoyance at the missing hair and laughter at how odd it looked.

"I don't know," John answered. "I think I felt him touch my head back there, but I didn't think anything of it."

I sighed heavily as I asked, "Did you notice if he turned on the razor? Because there are two bald spots back here and I can't cover them up."

"Oh, I didn't know he had the razor," he said. "Does it look okay?"

"It looks like someone shaved your head bald in these two spots," I said. "I'll do the best I can to cover it up, but your hair is going to look funny for a couple of weeks."

I finished his haircut as best I could and then we both laughed at the silliness of it all. Somehow, John-John had figured out how an electric razor worked and then removed the hair guide from it so it would shave at the lowest level. He ran off giggling after he finished the deed. Fortunately, hair grows back and, after a couple of weeks, John's hairline was near normal again. While we had many difficult times with him, there were times when he acted like any other child. It would have been so much easier if John-John's other issues had been as simple to solve as the computer switch, but it was not meant to be.

Resources, References, and Reflections – Parent Support for Autism

When John-John was a toddler, we did not yet have a diagnosis for autism, but John and I were coming to grips with the fact that our son was not like other children. I remember grieving as the reality sank in and I realized that he had a disability that did not show up until he was older. I was oddly envious of parents who know of a disability when their child is born. During John-John's first few years, there were many frustrations, which is normal for any parent, but also a feeling that he would eventually grow out of these behaviors. With a diagnosis of autism and the grim outcomes of the time, it felt like I had been living a lie and that there was little hope for our son to have a normal life. I resisted this idea and I did not want to accept that my son would eventually need to be put into an institution, hidden away from the world. I knew that some parents had started taking care of disabled children at home, such as children with Down syndrome, so I felt that we could do something to help him.

When we tried to work with the pre-school, part of me hoped that there would be an easy solution and our son would be helped and become a normal child. But a part of me mistrusted professionals in this field. I wanted to believe that there was a fix, but in the end I felt that my husband and I knew as much or more, and could do more, for John-John on our own.

I would experience great difficulty in choosing a different path due to my mistrust, anxiety and lack of confidence when working with institutions and their rules. I felt I needed to be a strong advocate for my son, but I also knew that I would back down and not speak up in direct confrontations. I do not react quickly in confrontational situations and I still have problems with speaking up about problems as they occur. If there had been better and additional choices in the pre-school community at the time, perhaps we could have found a match for our situation. But we did not have the resources to work with. I began researching autism at this point, doing my best to find positive outcomes, but it took several months for me to dig out any real content in our local library and the little research I could find on-line at the time.

While there now exists a greater understanding of autism, it can be overwhelming because there are so many choices. A stigma still hangs over autism and the portrayal of a grim outcome for the children if they aren't helped. In my opinion, the movie *Rain Man* helped with autism awareness, but the ending enforced the idea that autistic people will eventually be institutionalized. There are many therapies for early intervention, depending on the people parents work with when their child is diagnosed. The interventions can consist of speech therapy, assisted behavioral analysis (ABA) therapy, relationship development intervention (RDI) therapy, and occupational therapy. A parent can visit with professionals and have choices for therapy to help reach their child. There are also more positive images in the media, including the movie about *Temple Grandin*, *Life, Animated* and *Po*. As I write this book, *Sesame Street* has added an autistic character and other movies, such as the *Power Rangers* have announced that they will include an autistic character as one of the rangers.

However, all of these treatments cost money, and parents must try to gain financial aid through their health insurance or state agencies. In the meantime, they still have to deal with the behavior of their child and may have to endure months on a waiting list before they receive any help. Respite care for parents is available, but may be limited or not meet their needs. Assessing and choosing from among these options can be challenging and add the stress of feeling that the wrong choices may doom the child to a lifetime of solitude in their own world.

In addition, the current resources from state agencies, schools and insurance are scarce, and parents must sometimes be willing to become warriors to obtain adequate support for their situation. There can also be a great deal of pressure to accept a solution that works for the agencies, but which causes additional stress in the family because of how the child is treated.

Parents have to deal with their feelings about their dreams for their child and how those dreams have to change. To me, this period resembles mourning for the child they thought they wanted and might feel that they have lost. Based on my experiences, the parents should also look for support and help as they work through their feelings about not having the normal child they expected. It might help to understand that parents of normal children also need help from time to time when their child runs into difficulties. Parenting children to be responsible adults is a tough task for anyone and problems that seem huge when a child is a toddler or preschooler can change as the child grows.

I have found a list of resources from parents and groups that may help as they try to figure out what autism is and how it will affect their family. I wish that I had been able to find some support from a parenting group so that I would have known our family was not alone with our issues.

Asperger Syndrome & High Functioning Autism Association – www.ahany.org

Autism Highway – www.autismhwy.com

Autism New Jersey. Autism New Jersey. n.d. 2 October 2015. www.autismnj.org.

Autism Research Institute. n.d. 2 October 2015. www.autism.com

"Autism Through the LifeSpan." *Autism Society*[3], n.d. Web. 2 October 2015. http://www.autism-society.org/living-with-autism/autism-through-the-lifespan/

Disability Scoop. n.d. 2 October 2015. www.disabilityscoop.com

Meetup.com – http://www.meetup.com/ – search for local support groups for autism.

"Resource Guide." *Autism Speaks*[4]. n.d. 2 October 2015. https://www.autismspeaks.org/family-services/resource-guide

---

[3] The Autism Society is one of the oldest support organizations for autism. It was founded by Bernard Rimland, a researcher of autism and parent of an autistic son.

4 The Autism Speaks organization does not have a good reputation with autistic adults however many families feel they have received help and support so I am including a reference for families looking for help.

5

Getting to Know Our Son – All Over Again

John

After our experience with the pre-school, we began to look at alternatives for J.T. In the early to mid-'90s, research was performed the old-fashioned way–libraries with card catalogs and reference books. The Internet was brand-new and only accessible by connecting to a telephone line. For those of us way out in the middle of nowhere, this meant long-distance charges. We had CompuServe, one of several pay services similar to the old AOL 2400 baud dial-up system. Information on autism was available, but not very much. It cost money we didn't have to use CompuServe along with long-distance charges to reach the nearest dial-up number, so our usage was limited to family e-mails and a little research on forums they hosted. It's different nowadays. An online search under "autism" yields more than 19,000,000 sites that run the gamut: forums, professional opinions, parents raising children with autism, and people with autism. In the early '90's, we were limited to print books or occasional messages in forums online.

Tammy found three books that provided some semblance of hope: *Thinking in Pictures,* by Temple Grandin, *There's a Boy in Here: Emerging from the Bonds of Autism,* by Judy Barron, and *The Sound of a Miracle,* by Annabel Stehli. All three provided some optimism that children diagnosed with autism could grow and thrive and live their lives away from an institution. They also let us know that we weren't alone in dealing with this problem. But even these books didn't offer much guidance to help an autistic child communicate. In each case, the families had found different solutions to reaching their children. In recent years, I've heard the saying, "When you've met one person with autism, you've met one person with autism" – which is to say, not all people with autism behave or react the same way to the various teaching methods. Those books confirmed this idea and we knew that we needed to find our path for reaching J.T.

The only common theme involved spending time with our son and making sure he interacted with someone on a regular basis. Since Tammy and I were always at the motel, we had the time, but it was so frustrating to try to work with J.T. With normal children, parents know that you have to repeat things as a child learns how to accomplish a task. The parent may have to repeat instructions several times, but eventually the child will catch on, usually within a few days. The child may regress at times or act out and not follow instructions, but sooner or later, some kind of understanding and communication is established.

With J.T., we would repeat the same instructions many times day after day and never get the same results. Sometimes he would seem to understand what we said, but most of the time he would just ignore us. Only if we kept the instructions very simple–shouting one or two words–would he sometimes remember and do the things we wanted. But when it seemed like he didn't want to do something, he would experience what is now called a meltdown. At the time, we thought it was a tantrum and he was simply acting out. As we researched, we understood that he was undergoing a meltdown because he was having problems in communicating with us.

In a meltdown, the child shuts out the environment due to the stress of dealing with extra input and demands on their attention. The child makes noise, moves or engages in other activities to soothe the brain and to try to cope with the situation. In these instances, the child acts out for many minutes, cannot be calmed and may react violently to any interaction. I can see that J.T. could not understand us, and he was overwhelmed by our repeated shouting. He would be okay for the first part of the day, but by the afternoon, when we tried to get him to do something, he would act out, crying and screaming, falling to the floor and not interact with us at all. His meltdowns would normally last about 20-30 minutes and he would have at least one each day when he was about two years old.

Meltdown seems like a better description, because a tantrum implies that the child is upset and may be acting out, but that he will stop if he gets his way. During a meltdown, the child screams uncontrollably. There is no interaction with people and it doesn't necessarily stop in short order, even if you try to give the child his way. Sometimes we would try to give in to him, but it would not help to calm him down; he would continue to lie on the floor and scream while we stood by and helplessly watched. We learned to let these meltdowns run their course and to stay close by to make sure he wouldn't hurt himself. We learned that we had to wait for him to calm down after he had worked through his frustration. It was only later, as we began to learn about autism, that we figured out he was merely frustrated because he didn't understand what we wanted him to do.

As the year passed, we had to deal with other issues. The motel brought in enough to pay most of our bills and living expenses, but it didn't cover everything. His hospital visit didn't help us, either. Our health insurance charged a $1,000 deductible and our premiums increased as well, so we raised our deductible to $5,000 to keep our premiums down.

To get by, we borrowed money on credit cards and the debt began to pile up. We needed another income, but nothing turned up in that regard. Over the next year, after J.T. turned three, I applied for some software development jobs and Tammy applied for an office position, but neither of us got a job offer. Opportunities were few and far between in the sparsely populated community of Greybull, Wyoming. We even got a Sunday paper from the closest big city – Billings, Montana – to look for work, but no software positions were available there, either. I remember applying for one software job and going to an interview. The job was about a two-hour drive from our home-through mountains-so it would have been a challenging commute during winter. However, other people applied for the job who lived even further away, which showed how few software jobs were available in the area. When people from a 300-mile radius apply for a job, that is definitely some stiff competition to overcome. Our only source of job listings were newspapers and we didn't have the money to subscribe to all of them in the surrounding area.

Our financial situation had always been precarious during those times and, as so precisely stated by Roger Miller in the song *Dang Me*, we always "spent the groceries and half the rent, and lack fourteen dollars havin' twenty-seven cents." We watched our money come and go all too quickly, and the previous winter's hospital bill for J.T. only made it worse. We just never seemed to have what we needed when we needed it.

Our lack of money continued well into the winter of 1993-1994. We had decided to keep the motel open that winter, but our income was much lower than the summer. Most of our rentals were to local businesspeople who needed weekly rentals. Our kitchenette units were popular, but in order to compete with apartments, we had to lower our rents. We did keep costs down by doing all of the cleaning ourselves during the winter, but the money from the summer months did not stretch far enough to make it through the cold season.

Even though we continued to keep a close watch over the classifieds, none yielded anything promising. By then, I had begun to look at all job openings–since the ad section wasn't very big. Then I noticed an ad for truck drivers. They offered to teach people how to drive a semi-rig and guaranteed the successful graduate a job with a moving company. After much discussion and many concerns, Tammy and I agreed that it would help if I drove a truck for the summer while she ran the motel and looked after J.T. We knew it would be tough on both of us, but I hoped to be routed through Wyoming so I could still see my family. This was the only job available, so I ended up applying and I was accepted for the school.

J.T. was still behind in his speech development. One or two words strung together were all he could seem to muster. However, his behavior was improving and it was a little easier to communicate with him. We had begun to understand each other a little better, even though he couldn't communicate with us. Most of the time, he didn't use words, though. He would either point or take us by the hand to what he wanted to do, then he would point to the object. His meltdowns occurred less often but it was painful for all of us when he had one.

"You Don't Want to Go For a Ride"

In the spring of 1994, I went to Billings for lessons to drive a tractor-trailer truck. I drove the country roads of Montana while my instructor sat beside me and clenched his teeth. You truly have to be a brave soul to take on a student driver in an eighteen-wheeler. I was really nervous, too. I gripped the wheel so tightly that my hands would ache. I would take one hand off the wheel and then the other, and shake them out to alleviate the pain. The instructor didn't know what I was doing at first, so he commented, "You're the friendliest person I have ever met. I've never known anyone that waved at cows before."

After a few weeks driving the backroads of Montana and Wyoming, it was time for my driving test. As part of the exam, I was supposed to back the big rig through a small maze of traffic cones. I think I hit almost every one, but the guy who administered the test gave me the "thumbs up." Suddenly, I had my first commercial driver's license. I drove that year for the moving company and lugged furniture across the country for people who were relocating. That left Tammy to deal with J.T. by herself.

My training didn't take too big an emotional toll on the family. I could see Tammy and J.T. on weekends. It also gave Tammy a chance to get used to running the motel without my help. However, the time for me to start driving came all too soon. I passed the commercial driving test and the moving company provided a rig. When I got my first assignment, Tammy reassured me that she could handle the motel and J.T. at the same time, but it was still tough for us to say good-bye.

For a while, I enjoyed driving for a living, because I got to see all of our family members. My mom lived in Arlington, Texas at the time, and Tam's parents lived in Houston. I drove all the way from Binghamton, New York to San Diego, California and, as they say, "all points in between." In fact, I got to see nearly all of the contiguous United States–plus, it gave me a break from having to deal with J.T. Meanwhile, during that summer, Tammy was stuck at home running the motel and raising our son.

It turned out that I would drive everywhere in the country *except* Wyoming. I became very familiar with the eastern states. I would call Tam at least once a week to make sure she hadn't pulled out all of her hair trying to deal with J.T. and the motel, too. She seemed to be doing fine. With each new load, I would hope for a route through Wyoming or Montana, but the moving company decided not to send me anywhere near Greybull.

That summer went by quickly and we were able to make some headway on our bills. The motel was doing well and I sent everything I made to supplement the motel income. Tammy had hired some help and was faring all right with J.T., but by mid-summer we were both ready for me to come home. The final straw came when I talked to another driver who went through training the same time as I did. He had already driven routes through Montana and Wyoming twice, so naturally I felt like my requests to be closer to home were being ignored. The time had come for me to take action.

After mulling over my options, I quit the trucking job in the middle of August of 1994 and took a three-day bus ride back to Greybull. After a mechanical breakdown on the last leg of the trip, I finally made it to the Billings bus station, where Tammy and J.T. picked me up. Tammy and I were glad to see each other, but for some reason J.T. didn't want anything to do with me. This came as quite a surprise, because he had always been comfortable with me. Now he just turned away and didn't even want me to hold him. However, about halfway back to Greybull, he decided that he was okay with me and sat on my lap, where he slept for the rest of the ride. I think he may have been upset with me for leaving, but he seemed to get over it relatively quickly. When he did curl up in my lap, I felt like I was finally home.

Tamara

During the summer of 1994, I managed the motel while John worked his trucking job. I hired a couple of high-school girls and an older lady to help out with the cleaning and laundry. With this extra help, I had coverage for John's portion of the work. This also gave me time to watch John-John between my rounds. I think that was the first summer that I cleaned rooms instead of doing laundry. John had usually cleaned rooms before, but now that he was on the road all the time, it was up to me.

Since I had the extra help and John-John was older now, I didn't have to check on him as often. I alternated days with one of the girls between the laundry and the cleaning to provide some semblance of variety. In between, I would check on John-John or he would come out and see how I was doing while he played. John and I had done the heavy cleaning during the winter, so I had time to train the new help that spring and early summer. We gradually established a schedule, and by July we were filling up and staying busy on a regular basis.

In the afternoons, I would spend time with John-John. We stayed cool in the house while I folded laundry and put it away for the next day. I would spend some time with him, usually helping him with the computer or some of his games. In the evening, guests stopped by the front office to check in, so I would leave the living room, check them in, answer questions and perform other activities as needed in the front office. John-John would watch TV or his videos when I worked while checking in with me every now and then. The first part of the summer was quiet and we saw no unusual guests or events.

During our busy season, I did my best to interact with John-John. I read books about autism and browsed forums on CompuServe to try to figure out what John and I could do to deal with our son. I don't remember where I got my first reference, but I do remember reading *Thinking in Pictures* by Temple Grandin and *There's a Boy in Here* by Judy Barron and her son, Sean, in point-counterpoint style. It was a story of life with him and his autism. His mother described their experiences, and Sean provided his memories and reasons for his behaviors.

"You Don't Want to Go For a Ride"

After reading about Sean's behavior as a young boy, I was given hope that we could reach John-John. But it was very frustrating to try to communicate with John-John, because the things that seemed so simple to me just didn't make any sense to him. He knew how to speak, but only used one- or two-word sentences. He had memorized many different companies' logos, but when I'd tell him to do something or not do it, he would run off or throw a tantrum if I kept trying to get him to do a specific task. At these times, I suspect I sounded to him like one of the adults in the *Charlie Brown* cartoons and John-John would show frustration that he couldn't understand what I was saying.

Sometime during the busy season, I learned to relax a little and not try to force him to do things exactly as I wanted him to. We both missed John and the buffer he provided in our interactions. John-John and I had become quite frustrated with each other, so I felt it was better to let go of my expectations, because it certainly wasn't helping either of us. Then, after reading *Thinking in Pictures*, something clicked for me. I felt that John-John's problems were based on the fact that he saw things but didn't know how to connect words to them. I thought that if he could draw and hear the words spoken that he could use the pictures to communicate.

However, this turned into another area of aggravation for me—just trying to show him how to draw became an obstacle in the learning process. I brought out water-colors, crayons and colored pencils in an attempt to show him how to draw and then write the words to describe the pictures. I also repeated the words as I pointed to each image that I drew. Sometimes John-John would sit and watch, but mostly he would lose interest and run off to play with his toys.

During those summer afternoons, after the rooms were cleaned but before guests started to check in, I would sit at our kitchen table with various drawing materials. I would spread them out on the table and draw stick figures while trying to get John-John's attention.

"John-John, look, here is a house," I would say while I drew the picture. "See the house? Can you draw a house?" Then I would point to a specific feature in the drawing. "John-John, here is the door. House, John-John, house. Try to draw a house." I found myself repeating phrases, as I had repeated his name, in an attempt to get an indication of his interest in my words and the drawing. I would sit him down at the other end of the table with toys and try to capture his interest while I drew. Sometimes I gave him paper and he would scribble while I drew and described what I was drawing.

This began a repetitive cycle of words and pictures. "Here is the window," I said while drawing the square on the side of the stick house. "Here is the chimney, just like ours. See, John-John?" I said while tapping the square and triangle I drew for a chimney on the top of the house. I would also draw scribbles coming out of the chimney to represent plumes of smoke coming out of the top. "John-John, look, house, see the house. John-John, house, draw a house." Occasionally he would look at my work, but most of the time he would hum and scribble on his paper.

"John-John, look, this is a cat," I continued. "See the cat? Can you draw a cat?" I would draw a circle for the face with eyes, pause, then draw a body, stick legs and a tail sticking out of the back. I would tap on the picture and say, "Here is the cat's head, John-John. See the head. John-John, see the eyes?"

When I finished the drawing, I pointed to every part. "John-John, look, here is the body. Kitty says 'meow', kitty purrs." Sometimes I would write the words under the body parts. "John-John, look, see the kitty? Like our kitty? Can you draw a kitty-cat?" He would either scribble or look around, not seeming to pay attention. He might stare at the drawing for a moment, but he would always look away. Then he would run off, humming as he went. After this happened when he came back, I would use only one or two words, instead of an entire sentence. "Kitty-cat," I would say and then point to my stick figure drawing of a cat. Then I would draw eyes and say "kitty-cat's eyes" and point to them. He would sit and listen, then eventually run off again. We had a cat at the time that John-John was fond of, so I thought maybe he could connect the picture of the cat with the orange-striped cat he liked to carry around the house.

Another day would bring another drawing. This time it was a car, one of his favorite things. "John-John, see the car, here is a car," I prompted. "Can you draw a car?" I would draw circles and say, "John-

John, here are the wheels. John-John, see the car. Here is the window."
I would draw a square on the side of the car and tap on it as I showed
him the window I had drawn. I would repeat, "John-John, here are the
wheels, here's the door, here's the steering wheel. Can you draw a car?"

He would sit for a while and listen to me as he scribbled on his
paper, very focused and not looking at me, but he would always change
his focus to something else while he listened. He might look for a
moment, but he would always go back to his paper. Eventually, all of
these sessions ended with him running off and humming. I still
remember my sense of defeat in not being able to connect with him
and in not receiving any responses to my questions or direction.

I remember one afternoon very clearly. We sat at the table with
John-John at one end kneeling on his chair and hunched over a sheet
of paper while I sat by him. He used crayons on drawing paper and I
drew shapes on a tablet of drawing paper while he scribbled. I repeated
his name and pointed to the paper and named the objects as I had done
so many times before. But he never looked up. He just scribbled as I
talked. Eventually he started to hum, got up from his chair and ran
back to his room. Again, as I had done so many times before, I held my
head in my hands as my tears fell to the table and I asked myself, "How
can I reach my son?" I now realize that his humming was a method of
stimming, but at that time I did not know anything about these
behaviors and how autistic people use them to calm themselves when
they are highly anxious. I could see that my son wanted to please me.

When I asked him to draw, he scribbled on his paper, but he never connected the shapes I drew with something he could draw, too. I now realize that he was probably humming so he could reduce his anxiety and still stay with me at the table. Eventually, the anxiety for him would grow so much that he would have to run away and burn off his nervous energy before he exploded into another meltdown.

I had worked with other four-year-olds who could understand and take direction for their drawing, but my son never seemed to comprehend or make the connection between the pencil, the images and the objects they represented. Sometimes I would lay my head on the table and weep because I felt like a failure in not being able to reach him. My depression would cause me to lose interest, so some sessions would be days apart. On the plus side, the motel was running smoothly. However, I realized very little progress in reaching our son. I continued drawing and I practiced after John-John would run off. I even sketched him one afternoon as he napped. It was the only time he stayed still long enough for me to sketch how he looked.

Sometime in August, John and I became fed up with not seeing each other and I felt that John-John missed his daddy – even if he couldn't tell me about it. His father had been his big buddy and it wasn't the same without John around the house. Toward the end of the month, John quit his driving job and caught a Greyhound bus back home. I swear those three days John spent on that bus were some of the longest I've ever known. After a very quiet and uneventful summer, it seemed like all of the problems decided to visit during that time. The first day began with a broken water heater that flooded the laundry room. However, since that water heater only supplied the laundry, we were still able to assist our guests on that side of the motel. I found the flood in the morning and I was able to get a plumber to come out that day to replace it, so it was more of an annoyance than a problem.

In the meantime, while waiting for the plumber, I realized that another guest had somehow managed to stuff a water glass into his room's drain and stop up the toilet. Fortunately, when the plumber came over to replace the water heater, I asked him to check that room. I was amazed when he pulled that glass from the pipe. I still have no idea how he was able to get that inflexible glass down the pipe without breaking or cracking it. That guest also paid with a check, which bounced after I deposited it. We didn't accept checks often and that was the third check that had bounced. John called the other two people and they eventually paid, but this person couldn't be found. That was one of only two bills that we didn't get payment for—probably a good record for the four years we had run the motel. That afternoon, I was annoyed but I thought that after an uneventful summer, these incidents weren't too surprising. I figured that would probably be the worst I would have to deal with before John came home. Little did I know of the trouble that would show up that very evening.

The problems continued through the night on that first day when a car drove up that looked like its occupants might be a problem. Over the years, John and I had developed a sense for how certain guests would act. While we didn't establish long-term relationships with our guests, we did see a lot of behavior – good and bad – because we had to clean up after them. The kinds of problems people could cause amazed us at first, but after four years at the motel, we had learned a lot about guests and the likelihood of what they would bring during their stay.

For example, older couples were usually neat and clean, but also interested in some kind of discount. There was also a 50/50 chance that the couple would ask for a room with two beds for two people instead of a room with just one bed. For families with children, there was usually some kind of mess, although one family with eleven children stunned us as they left the room very neat. If the car looked older or beat up, the people in it, young or old, tended to be messier in the room. I don't know that I could name all the things we looked for, but we had a lot of experience in making quick judgments of guests and what they might be like during their stay. That evening called on my experience yet again. A small car that just did not look right pulled into the parking lot. Most people just stayed one night. They weren't overly messy or excessively neat, just friendly strangers passing through. Others looked like they should have had "TROUBLE" tattooed on their foreheads.

This car was small, old, rusty and dented. From the office, I saw the driver talking to the passenger before he came in. After sizing them up, I had already decided that our maximum room rates would apply.

We were a AAA motel and we stayed within the rate structure we defined for them, due to the ad in the AAA book. However, the manual allowed some flexibility and we had some discretion in what we charged. I would stay within that range, but if someone looked like they might be a problem I would quote the upper end of the price spectrum. Other motels did not follow the AAA guidelines or would use other tactics to keep out undesirables during the busy summer months, but we did our best to keep our rates fair and within reason. However, sometimes the money wasn't worth the aggravation and since it was summer, it wouldn't be a problem for the motel to fill up if a person left because they didn't like the price quoted at the desk.

When a vehicle like this pulled up, usually quoting the maximum prices would result in the person changing their mind and driving off to find a room somewhere else. Since it was August and only mid-afternoon, I wasn't concerned about filling up and figured it wasn't worth it to have this guest stay with us. When the man entered the office, it just confirmed my initial opinion. He was dressed in very beat-up blue jeans that looked like they hadn't been laundered for a while, a baseball cap, and a striped cotton shirt that wasn't tucked in. He had a slight beard that looked scruffy and my initial impression was of someone who was a bit sloppy. When he asked about a vacancy, I said we had one and then quoted the high price for a room with two beds.

I expected him to say no thanks and leave to go look for another motel. I was disappointed because he and his friend had just come from

Cody and thought our high rate was a bargain. He told me that he was driving for his friend who had a prosthetic leg and that his friend was paying for him to take him across the country. I cringed inside, checked them in and wondered how messy they would leave room next morning. I didn't think much else of these guests. There had been similar types who had stayed with us and I knew we could clean up most messes without too many problems. After that, I went back to my other chores in the house while I listened for people coming to the front desk.

As the day wore on, more people stopped by to check in and keep me busy. I got calls at the front desk and guests stopped in to ask questions: where was the nearest restaurant, was there anything to do, how far was it to Mount Rushmore or Yellowstone. However, the fellow who had given me the bad feeling kept calling the front desk and asking for the best restaurant in town, if the bar across the street was any good, or what stores were open at night. He also asked for an extra towel and some extra cups, which I took to his room. I was getting a little annoyed, but kept answering the questions, took down the items and worked to maintain a professional attitude. When I stopped by the room, the door was open, and the driver and passenger were sitting just inside the doorway chatting with each other and some other guests as they walked by. I noticed some trash spilled in the room and lots of cigarettes in the ashtray as I peeked in the room, and sighed about the next day's cleanup.

The final request of the evening from this guy was a cup of bleach for his dentures. That was certainly a new request, but we had plenty of bleach on hand for the laundry, so I filled a plastic cup and brought it to his room. This is where the situation went from annoying guest to outright creepy, and I confirmed to myself that he was possible trouble. When I came up to the room, the door was open and he was standing in the doorway. He was leaning against the door, arms crossed, almost as if he were trying to pose for a picture or for me. I handed him the cup, he said thank you and then he looked away from me, off into the sky. While he struck this pose, he said, "Well, that was really nice of you. You seem like a nice lady. If you need help up in that office, you feel free to give me a call any time this evening, and I'll come in and give you a hand." He continued looking off, maintaining his pose against the door jamb, a slight smirk on his face as he slowly drawled his offer.

I don't remember what I said. It was something like I didn't think I would need any help. I think I may have mentioned that my husband could help me out if needed. I walked quickly to the front office, and felt a lot better when he was no longer behind me where I couldn't see him. I knew I didn't always read social situations correctly, but it seemed like he was trying to flirt with me and that he sensed I was alone up at the house. Since I really was on my own, except for a toddler and a small beagle, I didn't feel any better about the situation.

Within the hour, the motel had filled up, but I was happy because that meant I could close the office on time and not have to worry about waiting for additional business after regular office hours. Normally, I would lock up the place and leave the office lights on in case of late-night guests wanting to check in. I would also leave the blinds up so I could see through the glass door. This time, I remember anxiously watching the clock. I was afraid that strange man would make another call or come into the office. At precisely 10 p.m., I slammed the door, turned off the office and motel sign, and closed for the night. I was really glad that man didn't come back to the office or make another call, but after that weird encounter earlier, I didn't want to take chances on our office looking open when there were fewer people around. I sighed with relief, got John-John and myself ready for bed, and headed off to sleep.

Later that night, I was awakened out of a sound sleep by the doorbell. It was a little after 2 a.m., but for some reason I was alert as soon as I heard the bell. I had a bad feeling and I knew then what it meant to have your blood run cold. My right arm felt frozen—as if a bag of ice had been strapped to it—and I had a very bad feeling about whoever was at the door. There was a restaurant/bar across the street from our motel and it would have closed at around two. Later, I think a part of me felt that the creepy guest had rung the bell after coming back from the bar. I froze in bed and debated about whether to get up. As part of our AAA status, we had agreed to man the front desk 24 hours a day, which meant that someone had to be available to get up for emergencies. My husband would usually take care of that, but for the first time I was the only one there to manage the place. The doorbell hadn't rung again, but I was concerned that this guy might be standing out there and might act up if I didn't check things out.

I finally unfroze after a few minutes and decided that I had to check the front door in case there was some type of emergency. I put on a robe, had a peek out front and fortunately didn't see anyone, either at the door or in our parking lot. I went back to bed, but it took me a while to calm down. This had been a very unnerving experience and I would be so glad to see those two fellows check out the next day.

My help showed up the next morning and we got most of the cleaning done, except for the one room. No surprise here – they would be a late checkout and, sure enough, fifteen minutes before their 11 a.m. deadline, I got a call at the front office. This was normal behavior for guests that needed a little extra time to check out. The guest said they had overslept and they would like to check out late. We usually didn't charge, but in this case I told him there would be a ten-dollar charge to check out an hour late. I had done this once before for a family of five, but when the father found out it would cost more to stay late, they cleared out of that room in record time. I had thought that charging extra might help to get them out sooner, but like the room rental, it didn't deter him and his friend. He asked again for some time, but I stood firm and he finally said they would pay the fee. I sighed in relief, but I relaxed too soon.

A little after 11, all the other rooms had been cleaned, so I made arrangements with two of the girls to come back later and help me clean up that room and get laundry put up. The help left and shortly afterward another guest checked in, which was unusual. Nothing scary about this guest, however, so I was happy to have someone else at the motel with me. I worked on the laundry and kept the laundry room door closed, in spite of the heat. The room was right next to these two troublemakers, and it just didn't feel safe to have the door open while he and his friend were still in the motel. The laundry room doors led to the front of the motel and to the back yard and our house. I closed the door to the front of the motel while leaving the back door open so I could get to the house quickly if I needed to. I did not want to take a chance on getting trapped in there if one of the two decided to come in while I was there.

About quarter to noon, while I was busying myself the phone rang and my heart sank. Sure enough, it was from the guests who wanted the late checkout. He wanted to stay another night and was checking to see if the room was available. My thoughts raced and I felt it would be bad news for him to stay another night, especially to be there all day while John-John and I were alone in the house. I told him that the room was unavailable and he suggested moving to another room if the current one was unavailable. Still thinking at top speed, I told him that

111

there was not another room available, that we were all booked up. He then started saying he didn't believe me and I repeated there was no room available for him that night. He started yelling at me, things like "how could I do this to him" and "I didn't understand him" and several other things that sounded like he thought I was a girlfriend and not a motel owner. He started getting louder and I could hear him yelling in his room through the laundry room walls. Then he told me that not renting him a room was illegal, and that he would call a lawyer and sue us if we wouldn't let him stay another night.

I normally would have folded and let them stay for the night, but some part of me felt this was a very bad idea. Somehow I kept calm after his threat of legal action. I said that if he didn't leave, I would call the police and have him evicted. Then I hung up the phone. I could hear him through the adjacent wall, screaming profanities in his room and how he wouldn't let me get away with this. I heard his door slam and then I really panicked. The laundry room was away from the house and the office, and John-John was playing in the house. He knew how to unlock the door and I was afraid that he would open it door for this crazy person. I vaguely remember flying past the back of the motel as I ran to the front office, certain that I would be too late and there would be a lunatic inside our home with my child.

When I got to the house, our little beagle was standing in front of John-John, hackles raised and barking at the person standing at the door while waving frantically. It was not the man who had creeped me out, but his friend who was traveling with him. He looked very worried and I vaguely saw a piece of paper in his hand. John-John was observing all of this and giggling at the barking dog, while the dog stood between him and the door. The dog and I knew this could be serious, and my adrenalin was pumping in full force. I pulled the dog back, but she kept trying to go through the door to get to him. He looked very worried as he waved a ten-dollar bill at me. Luck was finally on my side. I opened the door and he shoved the bill at me for the extra hour and pleaded with me to not "call the cops." They would leave without further incident. Through the whole ordeal, I held our dog by her collar as she tried to lunge through the opening at him. I told him that so long as they left within the hour, I wouldn't call the police. He left and I quickly shut the door, calmed the dog, and made sure John-John was all right. Then I collapsed behind the desk and started crying hysterically. I was so afraid that these guys were going to come back and break through the door.

In what turned out to be really good timing, John called me at just that very moment. He would normally phone me later in the day, but the bus had stopped for a break, so he took the opportunity to ask me how things were going. This was long before cell phones were common, so I did not have a way to reach him. He had to call while driving the truck or riding the bus back home. I sobbed out what had happened, but he spoke quietly and finally calmed me down. This took a few minutes, so I crouched behind the desk through the entire phone call. I had to remain hidden in case either of those men came back.

John then suggested that I call the motel owners down the street and to call the police. I was happy for the suggestion, because I usually don't think of asking for help, even when others might be glad to lend a hand. When I called the other motel, the owner helped to calm me down further. He was a former policeman and said he was ready to help. He also suggested that I call the police so they would be on alert if I needed them. I called them next and they offered to send someone down, but by this time I felt very foolish and thought I might be overreacting. I told the dispatcher on the phone that I thought I would be okay. There was another guest in the motel and I would stay in the office until I was sure I was alone, but they reassured me that they were ready to act at a moment's notice. I thanked them and said I would let them know how things went.

After a half hour, I peeked out a front window and I didn't see their car. I was still frightened, but somehow I forced myself to go outside and verify that the car was gone and not just parked in another space. I used my master key to open their room, readying myself to run in case they were hiding. The room was vacant, but it was a mess. Trash had been strewn about the place and the bathroom was soaked, but I found myself quite happy that this was all I found. I called the police and the other motel owners to let them know the problem tenants had gone.

An hour later, my help had returned to clean the room. By this time, I had completely calmed down and now felt like I had misread the situation. I didn't trust my reaction to the whole thing and thought it hadn't been as bad as I had imagined. I felt very foolish and I told this to my helpers. One of them said, "No, I don't think so. I saw that car and it had a bad feeling to it. I think you did the right thing." Her support helped me feel better, but I am really glad that it was the only encounter like that at our motel – or anywhere else, for that matter. Afterward, I half-expected to see them on a "wanted" poster in a post office or on "America's Most Wanted."

On the third day, I was very happy to drive up to Billings to pick up my husband. His bus was an hour late due to a breakdown, and John-John was fussy and impatient while we waited at the bus station, but after the events of the last two days it was very nice to have John back and our family together again. Even our son's autism seemed less of an issue.

Resources, References, and Reflections – Learning About Autism

As John and I adjusted to the reality of our son's autism, I renewed my research skills. I read as much as I could about the condition, looking for bits and pieces of hope that my son could eventually lead an independent life. In the meantime, we began to adjust to the fact that his meltdowns, humming and other odd behavior would not go away easily. However, a part of me still felt that if I did the right things, my son would respond and somehow become a normal child. I knew there was a person in there, and I just wanted to talk with him and learn more about what he liked. I wanted to share holidays with him and create good memories that he could look back on as he grew older. I had accepted this part of our new life, but I couldn't concede the entire situation as hopeless. I vowed that I would fight for him to get the most he could out of life.

I wish I had been able to find other parents to share experiences. I did attend a mother's group a couple of times, but I felt very disconnected from what the other mothers were sharing that I just couldn't continue. They told stories of their problems with potty-training, their child saying "no" and talking nonstop, or making messes. I had a child who I couldn't talk with, who showed no interest in potty-training, and who would run back and forth through the house and hum to himself instead of playing. I felt such a disconnect from other families that I felt isolated and out of place, so I stopped attending the meetings. It would have helped if other parents of autistic children were available to talk to and share stories.

I would have talked about how, after several months, I had learned that my son only wanted to wear green or blue shirts. Any other color would result in a tantrum – and I had no idea why. It took me a few months to figure that one out. Eventually, I was able to buy a bunch of green, blue and green-mixed-with-blue shirts that he could wear without screaming or throwing a tantrum. He wouldn't eat bananas, a fruit most babies love, but he would make a concoction of apple juice, milk and water and drink that right down. I definitely recommend that parents who are new to the diagnosis of autism seek out other parents of autistic children so they can share their experiences. Online blogs and forums are available so you can find out more information from parents who understand the challenges of raising an autistic child.

As our family gradually accepted the diagnosis of autism, we found our way of life changing. We learned to deal with unusual behavior and coped with the issues as they came up. The following links describe life with an autistic child. While it's not what parents expect, it can be rewarding even when things are most challenging. I would encourage parents to always look for the positive behaviors in their child. It is much too easy to focus on the negative aspects.

"6 Benefits to Having an Autistic Child." *Scary Mommy*. N.d. October 26, 2015. http://www.scarymommy.com/the-perks-of-autism/.

"I'm Not Sorry." *Huffington Post*. January 23, 2014. http://www.huffingtonpost.com/courtney-alison/im-not-sorry_b_4599233.html?utm_hp_ref=mostpopular.

"Let's Talk Parenting Taboos." *TED Talks*. December 2010. http://new.ted.com/talks/rufus_griscom_alisa_volkman_let_s_talk_parenting_taboos.

Speaking of Autism. n.d. Web. http://www.speakingofautism.com/.

"Superman is Autistic." *Autism Sparkles*. June 30, 2013. October 26, 2015.

http://autismsparkles.com/2013/06/30/superman-is-autistic/.

"The Perks to Having an Autistic Teen." *Scary Mommy*. n.d. October 26, 2015. http://www.scarymommy.com/the-perks-to-having-an-autistic-teen/.

6

Exploring Paths for Communication

John

The summer of 1994 was hard on all of us, and I was very glad to have returned home. I earned extra money driving and the motel had once again filled up, which meant we made good money over the summer. However, with credit card interest and our other bills, financial problems continued to hound us. The good news was that J.T. made progress while I was gone. Tammy had read the autism books and felt she knew more about why our son acted the way he did. She thought maybe he was similar to Temple Grandin in that he thought in pictures instead of words. Over the summer, she spent time drawing with him. At some point, something must have clicked, because in one afternoon he drew an entire stack of pictures based on a video game that Tammy liked to play on the Macintosh computer called *Lemmings*.

When she saw what our son had done, she continued to give him drawing paper, but she also went back to the Mac to look for graphic-drawing software. She eventually found a package called Kid Pix, a drawing program designed for kids. It works like Microsoft Paint, but with additional features and icons that a child can click on and put into a drawing without sketching items from scratch. She showed J.T. how to use the software and he took to it like a fish to water. Nowadays, iPads and tablets are available, but in the early '90s, children's software was sometimes difficult to use. Kid Pix used a different interface and J.T. was able to figure it out on his own.

He drew every day and that made all of us very happy. We finally began to see glimpses of how he viewed the world. He drew a big truck, which probably represented the rig I drove the previous summer. He also drew letters on the side of the truck—not entire words yet, but letters that meant something to him. He drew pictures of the motel and put people in them by using the icons or stamps in the program. He also used perspective in his pictures, which was unusual for a child his age—and the more he drew, the calmer he seemed to become.

We had finally found a path we could travel to see more of John-John's world. He used his pictures to communicate with us in a better way than just the few words he knew, and he could express some of his thoughts as well. This path was the first one we could all walk together. Not only did it let Tammy and I understand his interests, it allowed us to see what he thought about the world around him.

During the fall and winter of 1994-1995, J.T. spent a lot of time drawing on the computer and, as a result, he created a gallery of pictures. He also discovered Tam's *Bloom County* and *Calvin and Hobbes* cartoon books, from which he began to copy many pictures. He was really taken by the *Bloom County* series – especially the penguin, Opus. Tammy had bought a stuffed Opus doll many years earlier and put it into storage. J.T. found it and carried it everywhere. This new friend joined his cars when he played and he would move it around, along with some other stuffed animals as he played. We were encouraged to see him interacting with toys that were like people. Opus also appeared in many of his drawings as he practiced with the software.

Soon his drawings expanded in complexity: more realistic perspective, shades of light and dark, interior views and composition-all the things one would expect from an experienced artist. His drawings were very realistic. He also began to type words instead of random letters as he focused on this new tool.

However, with the stress of helping J.T. and trying to deal with our bills, we were both ready for a break. Around Christmas, we decided that we would drive down to Denver and take a few days off– just relax in the big city and try to distance ourselves from our problems. Unfortunately, the night before we were to leave, J.T. fell off the back of a dining room chair. He always liked to climb and was very good at balancing, so it wasn't unusual to see him crawling on furniture. It would scare us a bit, but he always got up and down safely on his own. This evening, however, was different. He lost his balance and fell to the floor. I tried to catch him, but I didn't make it in time.

He caught himself with his hand, but the force broke his elbow. Later, I was happy it was not his head but it was bad enough at the time.

J.T. began to cry and I took him into the other room where Tam was playing a synthesizer as she wore her headphones. I hollered that I thought J.T. might have broken his arm. She turned around, took one look and yelled for me to call 911. I called the paramedics so they could send an ambulance while Tam held John-John.

When the EMTs arrived, the ambulance attendant immobilized his arm, but until they put a bandage on the injury, he would not settle down. Since J.T. was little, bandages had been the answer for all of his "owies," so he had to have one. Tam rode with him in the ambulance while I followed. The 60–mile drive to the emergency room was longer than usual, but since the Greybull facility had closed two years before this, the closest decent hospital was in the West Park Hospital in Cody.

The hospital performed surgery on his arm, because the break was at the elbow. The doctor inserted two pins to mend it and made sure that the first cast was extra-tight, since he was a very active child. We did have one problem during this time: The doctors would not listen to us. When the first cast was replaced, we told them he would have to be sedated or he would struggle. They acted as if sedation was a new concept and they weren't willing to do it. With some misgivings, we allowed the doctor to talk us into holding down J.T. while the first cast was removed. However, when they put on the new cast, he screamed and struggled even though Tam and I, and one of the office nurses, restrained him. The doctor finally set the second cast, but he looked concerned and said he wanted to take an X-ray.

The film showed that J.T. had strained his arm enough to partially re-break it. They instructed us to bring him back in a week to see how things had set. When we brought him back, the doctor grimly told us he would need to re-break and reset the arm because it had healed wrong. So two days later, we brought John-John back to the hospital for another cast.

Unfortunately, after making an hour-long drive at 6 am, we found out his surgery had been delayed due to an emergency case the doctor was handling. By this time, we had a very upset four year old on our hands. We knew he would not sit still for an hour or more in a hospital room waiting for the surgery. The nurses said they wouldn't mind, but Tam and I realized that things would not go well if we tried to stay. The delay was only supposed to be for an hour or two, but it was another eight hours before the doctor was ready for the surgery. In the meantime, we drove around Cody, checking back every hour and tried to keep our angry, screaming child busy while we waited for the doctor to finish the other operation.

J.T. also wasn't supposed to eat, so on top of everything else we now had a *hungry*, angry, screaming child to entertain. The anesthesiologist still had to brief us on what would happen, but since our son was so upset, and Tam and I were both so worn out, we refused to budge from that van until they were ready to take him.

Fortunately, we were blessed with an understanding anesthesiologist. This doctor came out to our van, scrunched into a seat and patiently sat with us while explaining what would happen and how he would sedate John-John. When he saw how upset our son was, he offered to give him a shot at the entrance to the operating room. When they finally gave us the green light, I carried him in, the anesthesiologist gave him a shot to relax him, and I handed him over. Tam and I then waited for him to go to recovery and breathed a sigh of relief that he had come through just fine. Now he had a cast that he could wear until his arm healed. The good news was that this time, when we said he needed to be sedated before the cast was removed, there was no argument from the staff.

However, we now had another bill, and because of the high deductible on our health insurance, we owed the hospital $5,000. The doctor did waive his fee when he had to reset the arm, but that was the only bill we didn't have to worry about. We were just grateful that we didn't have to pay a double deductible. Since the accident had occurred right at the end of December, we were afraid that the insurance would reset in January, but the carrier didn't do that. However, that was the only saving grace while we dealt with J.T.'s broken elbow.

As our son's arm healed, Tam and I thought about how we were going to handle these new bills along with what we already owed. I looked into driving a truck again, locally this time, but my blood pressure had risen and I couldn't lower it in time to qualify for a commercial driver license. We looked at the ads, but like our previous job searches, there was nothing to be had in our part of the state. Tammy also looked for a job, but nothing showed up in the classified section in January of 1995.

Sometime just before J.T.'s fifth birthday, Tam had an idea: she would call her old boss down in San Diego to see if she could get some work. We agreed that if she could get a good-paying temporary job, I would run the motel and take care of J.T. Through the miracle of chance, her former employer had just received a new project the day before and was going to need help. It was due to start in a month, so we both waited on pins and needles for the confirmation.

Finally, two months after she began her job search, Tam was hired and started planning her move to San Diego. J.T. and I would stay at the motel and, just like the summer before, we would have extra help to handle the room cleaning. Tammy was able to stay until J.T.'s cast was removed, but all too soon she had to leave. She left without waking up J.T., I don't think she wanted to deal with trying to say good-bye to him when he didn't yet seem to understand everything around him.

J.T. showed little emotion when he didn't see his mom the next morning, but he did look around for her. He also indicated that he wanted to go see his grandparents, so we got into the car and took a drive. When we arrived at Tam's parents, J.T. looked around for her but didn't say anything. He just drew and played, but now something seemed a little off. After two months without Tammy, I hired someone to watch the motel for a while and we drove down to San Diego. It worked out well, because J.T. had missed his mother and his little face lit up immediately when they were reunited. It made my day, too. After their first separation and at five years of age, J.T. finally called Tam "mama." It made both of them cry. It was hard to tell, because I was leaking a few tears myself.

That was an interesting time for me—entertaining, even. One memory in particular about J.T. comes to mind. When we cleaned the motel rooms, we used to leave all the doors open and close each one after that room was finished. That way, we knew which rooms still needed cleaning. J.T. hadn't been potty-trained yet, but he knew the concept. He just showed no interest in using the bathroom on a regular basis. One morning, while we were cleaning rooms and all the doors were open, John-John ran stark-naked from one room to the next and peed in each potty. He would run into a room, pee a little, squeal gleefully and run into the next room to pee some more.

J.T.s behavior became more of a problem that summer. One tenant stayed with us for several weeks due to a shortage of housing in town. Since we had kitchenettes in some of the rooms, we provided an alternative for people who needed a little more than just a motel room. One morning, when I was out cleaning, I heard something that didn't sound right. I went to investigate and found J.T. with a handful of gravel from the parking lot wiping down this tenant's truck. I yelled at him to stop, and he took off. Fortunately, this tenant was understanding and wasn't too upset, but it certainly didn't make my day after finding him trying to wash someone else's car with gravel.

We had originally planned to take the money from Tam's temp job, have her come back and we would continue running the motel together—that is, until a man walked into the motel one day while she was still away and asked if the motel was for sale. About that same time, the people Tammy worked for offered her a full-time position. With these offers and the problems with some of J.T.'s behavior, we began to think about getting out of the motel business. We talked about it on the phone one night and came to an agreement: A higher power was telling us that we needed to move on—so we would sell the motel and move back to San Diego.

When I've had hard times, I get to a point where I am looking for some sign of what I should do to make things better. I don't always like the answer but eventually I can see the good that will come into my life when I take these hints. I believe this higher power has our best interests at heart. Sometimes you have to tune into that mindset for just a bit and take those hints. At any rate, we took the hint and turned the page to the next chapter of our life.

Tamara

Shortly before John came home from truck driving, I finally had a breakthrough in communicating with John-John. As previously described, I tried to show him how to draw on paper. After reading *Thinking in Pictures*, I felt as if I had increased my insight into how

John-John was thinking and why he had problems communicating. Over the years, I had pondered about my own thinking process and had a gut feeling that mine was similar to his. After reading Temple's book, I made connections and I believed that if I could make John-John understand the concept of drawing, he might gain another communication tool in addition to speech. Unfortunately, I had become very discouraged with him over that summer when he seemed to show no progress. He displayed no sign at all that he understood my words or the idea of drawing.

During the latter part of the summer of 1994, I again pulled out the drawing materials, but now I used an 11x17 pad of paper and watercolors. I had tried charcoal pencils, crayons and colored pencils, but nothing clicked with John-John. This time I used brushes with a glass of water and some napkins. I dipped the brush into the water and then into a color before I drew. John-John had always loved to play with water and I thought that maybe using water might get him interested in drawing.

"John-John, see the brush," I explained. "Put it in the water and then in a color. John-John, see, I'm drawing a train. Train, John-John." I then drew a train and said, "See the wheels, John-John. See the train? Choo-choo, just like the trains we see by the road." The town we lived in had railroad tracks running through it, so we would often see trains traveling through town. John-John always liked to watch them go by and he would say choo-choo when he saw one.

Then I drew a car and filled it in with the watercolors. "John-John, see the car. It's a red car. Vroom-vroom, fast car. John-John, car. See the wheels? Vroom-vroom, car." Cars were something else that he liked. He liked to ride in them and he also had a set of racing cars that he loved to wind up and race through a curved track. He seemed to listen while he put the brush in the water glass. He even tried different colors on his paper. I wrote his name on my sheet, then on his. "John-John, here's your name, 'John', John-John, your name – 'John.' Your name, John-John. See it?" I remembered that he knew his letters from the computer games. I just wanted him to see what it looked like.

While he was not imitating what I drew, he was using the brush and drawing lines across the paper. I felt that I was finally seeing progress with the new medium, so I continued to draw: a chicken and an egg, a fish, a telephone, a window, a feeble attempt at Mickey Mouse-anything to get his attention. My pre-school art can be seen below in Figure 1, while John-John shows his talents in Figure 2. I eventually got up to take care of laundry or someone at the front desk, but John-John stayed at the table and played with the watercolors. Perhaps the idea of being allowed to make a mess while I didn't get upset with him seemed like a fun new game.

I don't know what finally clicked, but while I worked in the laundry room, John-John took that brush and began to draw on his own. When I came back, I found that he had drawn lines across several different pages. I then watched him purposefully draw shapes as he moved the brush across the page, but it took me a few minutes to recognize his subject: characters from the video game *Lemmings*. He liked to watch me play, especially since some of the little creatures would splat and make funny noises. I found several drawings on the table that looked as if he were trying to capture images on paper as he imagined them. He had drawn lines, put them aside and then added more to the drawings.

Over the next couple of hours, he drew almost twenty pictures of different scenes from the *Lemmings* game. The drawings were crude, but since he had only drawn scribbles the day before, this was a huge step forward. He also captured details: the sides of the caverns that they wandered through, the feet on each tiny creature and subtle changes in location, as if they were actually moving. I remember feeling stunned as I looked at his pictures—and also a little numb at the notion that he had finally made some connection with the world through drawing a part of it. I felt a sense of joy that he could reach out to communicate with us.

After I finished with the laundry, I visited with my mother and grandmother. Since my parents were in town to visit, Mom and Grandma came over to visit John-John and me. I showed them one of his pictures and what John-John was doing. I exclaimed, "He's drawing! Look, this is from *Lemmings*, the computer game I play." Mom and grandma were very excited, because they knew of his difficulties in talking and with tantrums. After those early years of feeling as if I had failed my son, I had a sense of joy that I had finally been able to reach him in his world and help him reach out to our world. To me, this was the turning point where I felt that my son might communicate with us more and we could finally find out what he thought about the world around him.

I saved those first pictures, including one or two from when he just scribbled. The mix also consists of some that I drew in order to show him the concepts. These images depicted familiar objects and the corresponding words next to them. Some are little more than scrawling, where he just seemed to randomly move the crayon around the paper.

His watercolors began with one or two lines drawn straight across the page before he moved to the next one. But these were different—the lines had a purpose. Eventually, his drawings included a line drawn between two splotches. Finally he included splashes of color on the straight line that connected two other blots. As I viewed his work, it dawned on me that the line was actually a bridge that connected rocks, and the shapes on the line represented the lemmings crossing the bridge.

My son was drawing objects as he saw them. It seemed that he had finally found an alternate path to capture what he was thinking. The pictures he and I drew are included in the next section. I am still very proud of what he was able to accomplish on that summer afternoon when he was only four years old. This increase in communication was a big help in the next few months.

Figure 1 – Tamara's Sample Drawing for John-John to Copy

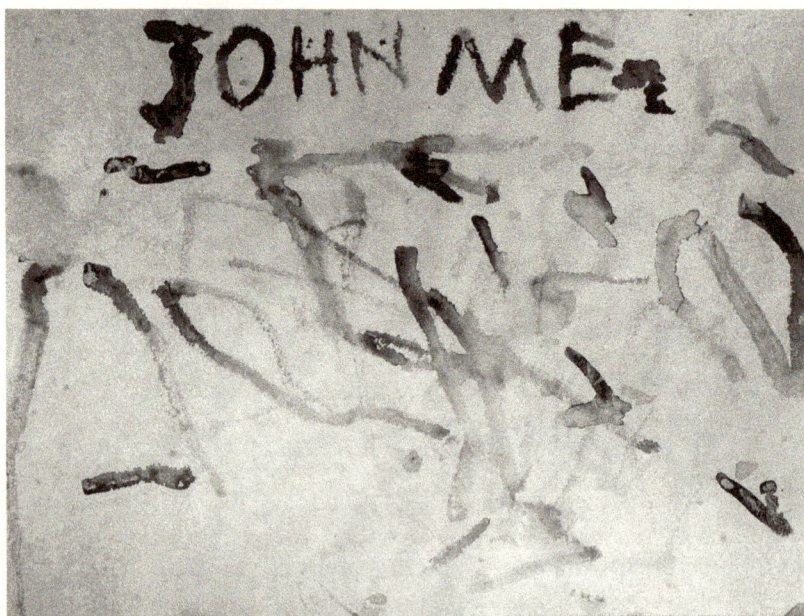

Figure 2 – One of John-John's Early Drawings

Figure 3 – One of John-John's First Purposeful Drawings

Figure 4 – John-John Adds a Figure to a Basic Line Drawing

Figure 5 – Lemming, Bridge and Details of the Cavern Below

Figure 6 – Lemming with Arms, Lava Erupting from Below

Figure 7 – Lava Above and Below the Lemmings

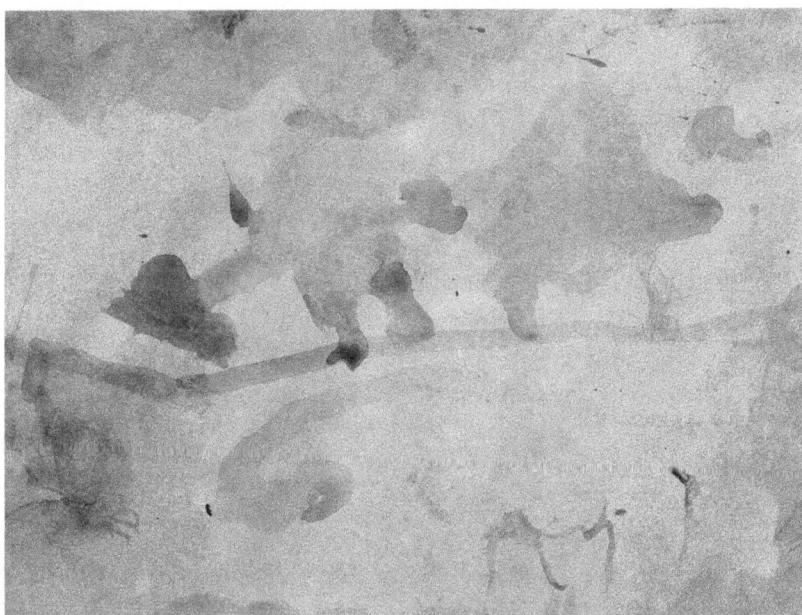

Figure 8 – Lemmings Crossing, Detail Above and Below

Figure 9 – Several Lemmings

During that fall of 1994, his drawing continued to improve, but I wondered if there were other media he could use to express his interest. We had an old Apple Macintosh computer and I found a program on it called Kid Pix. When I showed John-John how to use the software, he dived into it. He drew boxes with random letters and people stamped into the pictures. He had always liked computers and he had learned his alphabet on our PC. In that game, he could type a letter and the software would repeat the letter, a word that started with that letter and then show some animation about the item. He was very comfortable with computers and the new software was another way for him to stretch his imagination.

I soon realized that he was drawing the motel, and the guests and their cars. At first he just used random letters in the pictures, but gradually he began to use words that he could copy from the signs he saw around him. His naming process also changed. At first, he labeled his drawings with things like *ardhjkl..Jpg*, *157508977545-756564-67-8.jpg*, and one of my favorite drawings, *fjgngf fjrhryrf.jpg*. However, he somehow figured out that his letters could be used to spell words, so he started using names such as *signs.jpg*, *driving.jpg* and *chicken light on.jpg*. I think John or I offered suggestions on how to spell things, but John-John picked up many more words than either of us helped him with.

As he became more practiced, his drawings included more detail and realism. He also took an interest in my *Bloom County* and *Calvin and Hobbes* cartoon books. He would read through them and copy scenes from them into Kid Pix. He also began to add detail to his scenes: some with perspective, others cut off at the edges and more with advanced art concepts. They still looked like a child had drawn them, but they were more than that. One picture depicted me as a stick figure half-drawn in gray shades with the other half in color to show me standing between light and dark areas in a hall. The figures were normal for his age, but depicting light and shadow was a more advanced concept that he was expressing.

Over the next several years, John-John drew hundreds of pictures using the Kid Pix software. John and I included a few of them to show how his skill has changed during the different stages of his development. The Mac eventually broke down for good, but a friend rescued all of his pictures and gave them to me in PC format. This friend was a graphic arts and software major in college, and he was amazed at some of the techniques in John-John's pictures. He told me that several of these techniques had to be taught to high-school students. I was happy to hear this, but I was mostly glad that our son had found a way to communicate with us. He also began to add words to his pictures and even became calmer, now that he had discovered a way to express his thoughts. It was a big step – and also the first time I felt like our little boy might be able to come out into our world.

John-John would use colors in his drawings as well, so he drew my husband's eyes as blue. However, John-John would always draw large circles for noses. He was only three feet tall at the time, so we figured since he always looked up at people that his main view of their noses was their nostrils. In the late fall and early winter, before he turned five, he seemed calmer as he continued drawing on the computer. I had observed this calmness before. It always came about when he found his way through some difficulty, like learning to move as a baby or discovering a few words and basic communication with us when he was around three years old. This calm helped us a lot in the next few months, especially when he broke his arm, and John and I would suddenly have to make some tough decisions about our finances.

Figure 10 – File *fjgngf fjrhryrf.jpg*: A First Drawing in Kid Pix

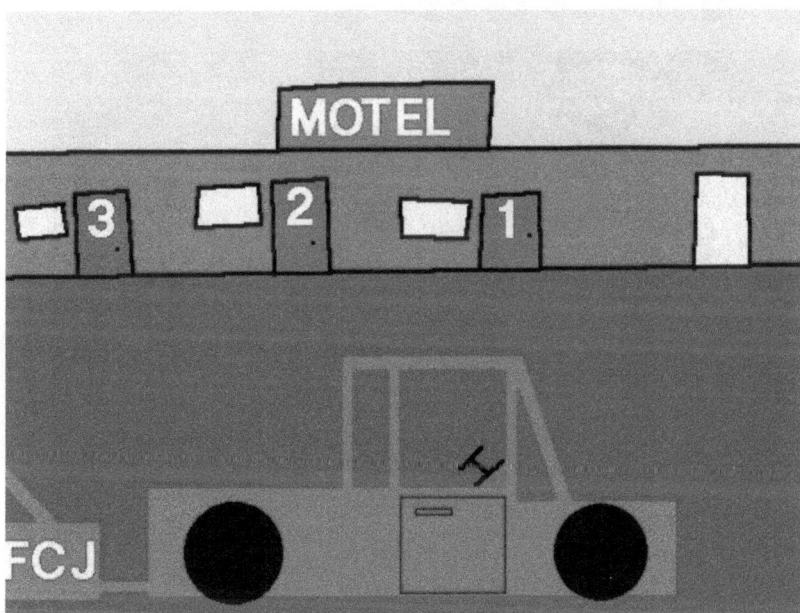

Figure 11 – File q*wbdefhhijklmnoq rstu.jpg*: Our Motel with a Car in the Parking Lot

John M. Harpster & Tamara Harpster

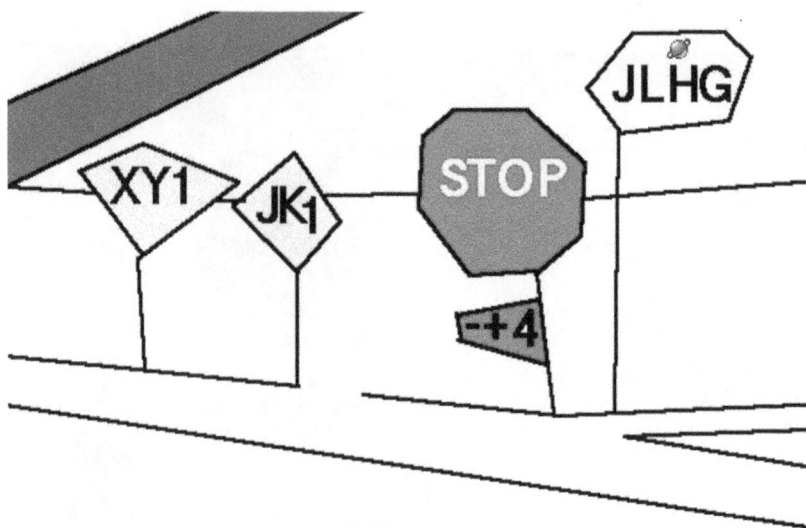

Figure 12 – File *signs.jpg*: Street Signs

Figure 13 – File *driving.jpg*: John and Me Riding in a Car

Figure 14 – File *chicken light on.jpg*: Copy of a Drawing from a Cartoon Book

Figure 15 – File *cozymamu.jpg*: Me Getting Ready for Bed

Figure 16 – File *dark in the kitchen.jpg*: The Three of Us during a Power Outage

Figure 17 – File *intersection.jpg*: Copied from a Cartoon Book

Figure 18 – File *mama & John-john's moon.jpg*: John-John and Me During a Full Moon

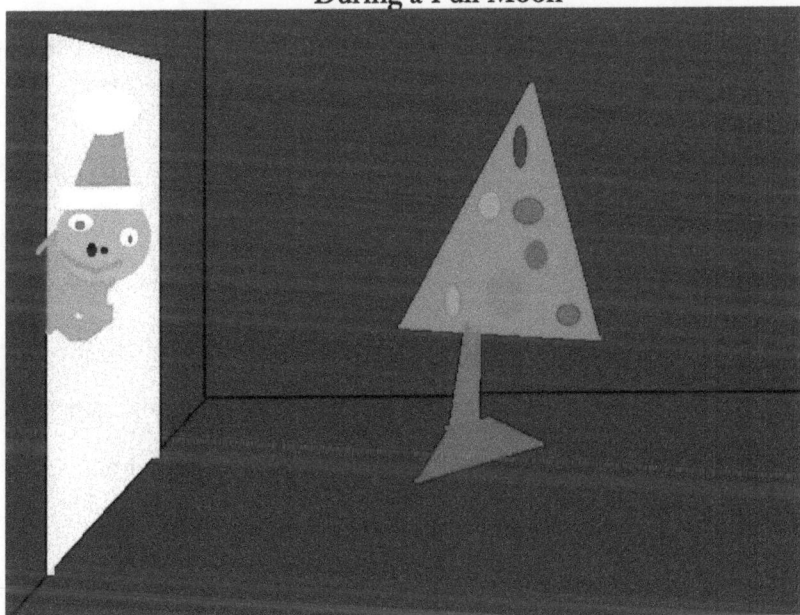

Figure 19 – File *MAMA CHRISTMAS HAT.jpg*: Christmas Tree with Me in the Doorway

John M. Harpster & Tamara Harpster

Resources, References, and Reflections –
Alternate Communication

Many autistic children struggle with verbal language, but speech therapy can help. However, I have found that just because a child can talk doesn't mean they are communicating. Even as John-John has gotten older, I have had to step back at times and adjust my communication with him. I cannot rely on just interpreting his words. I also need to read his body language, his facial expression and his mannerisms while he talks. When he says, "I don't want to go!" at the top of his lungs and while running back and forth, I can interpret that as meaning he does not want to go somewhere. If he says, "I don't want to go" in a normal tone while standing still in front of me and looking at me, it usually means he does want to go, but is not sure if I will say yes. Communication includes speech, body language and cultural assumptions that frame the context of conversations. In addition, for most people, there is a commonality in how people view things, so there is a shared thought process. This is apparent when certain jokes are shared about men and women, or when people talk about the current television shows or world events. Autistic people aren't always plugged into these common thinking patterns and may appear uninterested in normal conversation. When there are problems with speaking or reading body language, the body language and speech of autistic people may make them seem distance or remote, when they are actually very interested in the subject.

With electronic devices, some of these hurdles can be overcome, but again, speech or typing should not be considered complete communication. Think of the misunderstandings that can occur in e-mailing between two people where there is only text without the accompanying body language that frames a conversation. There can also be cultural differences – even within the same country – that can cause a misinterpretation of statements that seemed benign to the speaker.

Based on my experience, I think it helps if the parents can be flexible and focus on finding a way for the child to communicate how they feel, what items they want and what they need to feel comfortable. When John-John was younger, I was a lot less flexible. I expected him to tell me his needs and what he wanted. As I grew older, I had to learn to be more adaptable and reach more into his world, instead of expecting him to always figure out how to operate in mine. I have also built experience in understanding more of John-John's context and thinking patterns, so that I can translate them and try to understand him better. I find myself seeing him more as a person with his own thoughts and ideas, and less as a child that has to constantly be told how he should act and behave. This is how I act with other adults, accepting their differences just as they accept mine, and I have seen – in my opinion – that this is a more mature approach that yields better results.

When John-John was four years old and I was still struggling to reach him, I began to realize that I also think in pictures and images. Over the years, I have remembered incidents from my childhood when I realized I didn't think quite the same way as other children. One time in class, I pictured the knowledge coming into my brain, like boxes of cargo that were loaded onto a conveyor belt and were somehow moved into the space. As I sat in class, I smiled as I thought this and I drew a doorway on the side of my head with my finger. I then pictured the boxes moving into my head, with all of the knowledge from the books and the teacher talking to the class. Then I looked up, saw the teacher and other children looking at me strangely as I moved my hands around. So I stopped and looked down, ashamed that I was acting different again.

As an adult, I realized that I translate speech into thought patterns and vice-versa in order to carry on a conversation. This realization is part of why I feel that I am on the autistic spectrum. After so many years, it's mostly automatic, but when I'm overly tired or talking about new things, I have to focus or I lose my place and stutter, or just get stuck. If I'm near even a small group of people, I won't talk at all, because it's less embarrassing than stuttering or freezing up. If I am talking about a subject I'm not familiar with, there is a slight delay as I translate, which usually leads to a slight delay before I can respond. Since conversations can move from topic to topic very quickly, I find it very difficult to interact and keep up without breaking the rhythm of the group. This is another situation where I find it easier to stay quiet instead of feeling foolish or out of place – when I respond to statements that others have already moved away from.

Over the years, I have come up with a visualization of what it's like to try to communicate with someone who thinks in pictures, like my son or myself[1]. My memory is filled with images and movies of the world around me. This media has words associated with them that I can repeat when communicating with others – like assigning a value or a title to the image. The more comfortable I am with the process, the easier the words flow, but when I talk about new things, I fall back on memorized phrases to communicate my feelings. At times it is difficult to keep things short, because I have an entire movie that I want to describe, complete with sound, images, feelings, colors and smells, while most people only want to hear a sentence or two. I think it is similar to someone trying to tell of the entire plotline of a Shakespearean play in a 140-character Twitter post. It can be done, but a lot of information will be missing.

In order to overcome this difficulty and attempt to converse in a shortened form with others, I tend to use many quotes in my communication. I'll have a complete image in my head of a concept,

---

[1] John and I talked over this section and he did not understand what I was trying to communicate, which is an example of my problem. He told me that I should sum up my thinking as follows: "You have what you want to say in your mind in pictures, and it is hard to translate that into a language that other people understand." I wanted to include his concise summary to help others who are trying to translate my description above.: -)

with pictures, feelings, sound and a time component, but when I try to describe what I am thinking, most people become bored—or worse, annoyed or angry. In order to communicate all of my thoughts, I need to repeat a lengthy monologue, while most people can share experiences with a sentence or two along with common thought patterns. The other problem I have is that I don't seem to have the same view of the world as other people. I will leave out portions of a description that seem obvious to me, while over-explaining other sections that people take for granted.

When I find a quote that summarizes my feelings, it is a real time-saver for my communications. While I researched autism, I discovered the term "scripting."[5] This is a very accurate depiction of how I take shortcuts in speaking with others. It's much easier to have a set of memorized phrases to fall back on, instead of continually trying to

---

[5] There are two types of scripting: echololia and social. Echololia scripting is the repetition of phrases that may or may not fit in with the current conversation. The quotes are direct from movies, cartoons, songs or other media and are repeated in order to have a way to engage verbally with others, and to provide comfort to the person using them. In this way, the scripting is similar to stimming. Social scripting is when the autistic person uses a set of phrases or quotes that they can repeat for certain specific situations and reduce their anxiety of having to come up with a response on the fly. The aim of this type of scripting is to increase the range of engagement with other people in ways that are more socially acceptable. Unfortunately, the repetition or quotes can appear rude or annoying, and is frowned upon by many non-autistic people. When autistic people realize that they are annoying other people, this can raise their anxiety level, which can then increase the amount of scripting used by the person. In this video, the young, autistic woman, Amythest Schaber, explains the two types of scripting. It was interesting to note the same types of pauses in her speech that I have when I am talking about some new topic or talking with someone who I don't know. https://youtu.be/vtbbmeyh5rk. .

come up with new words. For example, when my son was 8 or 9 he became fascinated with a story about a person who had tied balloons to a lawn chair and accidentally rose to the altitude of 15,000 feet when he untied his chair from the ground. For months, John-John would go around repeating the phrase "Lawn chair Larry" and giggling with delight about this odd story.

Until a friend pointed this out to me, I was oblivious to the impression it gave. I came across as a know-it-all, when all I really tried to do was use it as a shortcut or to back up my ideas, because people really didn't want to listen to my monologues. However, as a result of this feedback about using quotes, I'm now self-conscious when I use them. This adds to my anxiety level when communicating with others. I'm already apprehensive, because I don't read behavioral cues or body language the same way as others. I have learned to cope, but I pay a price with anxiety, overthinking social situations on and a reduced interest in communicating—unless I'm sure I can trust the other person. At some point, it might be interesting to try to capture in a book the various rules I've developed over my life. But I don't know that I have enough time left on this earth to complete that type of endeavor.

Now that I know about the possible impression quotes can give, I've added an "internal check" before I speak. This is a validation of what my immediate future behavior will be. Before I speak or act, I quickly run through previous situations in my mind to determine what I should say, what tone of voice is acceptable, and what body language I should portray. Is the other person showing signs of boredom, lack of interest, hostility, anger or frustration, or some other emotion that could cause the encounter to escalate in emotional intensity? After many years of this, the check is normally pretty quick, but I still experience some delay in response to new situations, and I am sometimes annoyed with myself for missing some piece of communication from the other person.

When I was younger, I had a much shorter set of internal checks, and I annoyed, frustrated, baffled and angered people much more easily. I now have a longer set of internal checks, but my memory is not perfect and my checks do not cover every situation that could come up when dealing with other people. Because of the negative interactions I have had in the past, up to the point of driving away people who I cared about, I find that I prefer to not interact in most social situations, unless I have to or I am very comfortable with the people and trust that they will show patience when dealing with my social slips. After social situations, especially if they have been lengthy and I am tired, I will review the situation in order to see where I overstepped or misinterpreted behavior in order to add another internal check for the future. In the last year or so, I have started to move away from this model because of the level of anxiety and fear for social situations. I have been helped by having a stable situation for the last few years, a set of friends who are mostly understanding and tolerant, and the ability to control the times when I have to be involved in these situations.

As an example, while writing this section, I pulled up a memory clip of being introduced to someone. The clip involves a scene with me approaching the person I am meeting. I see a generic person who I am walking toward in order to shake hands and introduce myself. As I approach, I retrieve additional pictures of other interactions and I assess the stance of the person: how they are dressed, whether an arm is coming up for a handshake, is the person smiling, are they looking me in the face or are they looking away? As they shake my hand and tell me their name, I focus on repeating my name while shaking their hand without grabbing too tightly and not holding on for too long, then backing away to an acceptable social distance. Because of the other inputs involved with body language, I now focus on repeating the name to remember it and also associate it with the face. I also work on imprinting the face in my long-term memory, because some faces blur for me and it is hard for me to make out that person later. Other faces are very distinct and I have no problem remembering those people later, although I may not remember their name. I repeat the name and the memory of the face so if I meet the same person again at the event, I have a better chance of using the right name. If I meet a person who reaches out for a hug, I realize a slight delay while I process the difference and decide whether I want to accept. Because I am not very sure of what is proper behavior, it is likely that I would accept the hug because I don't want to offend, even if I feel uncomfortable with that behavior. If I do hug the person, I monitor the situation to make sure I break the hug before it gets uncomfortable while trying to not break too soon. Most of the time I like hugs with people I know but I am still unsure of the proper protocol and I have to monitor my actions.

Because of my experience at the motel, I may try to engage the person by asking where they are from, what is their job, or do they have a family, depending on the type of event. Once I gain a piece of information, I try to connect the item with some of my experience and ask a question to try to get the person to talk about themselves. Once I can get a person to this point, it becomes easier to interact, because most people like to talk about things they are familiar with. When this happens, I can ease off on my constant assessment of the situation and nod in agreement, or say something to encourage the person to keep talking. While this may seem like common sense to many adults, it took me many years to build up these basics and to make effective use of them.

I continue to translate things people say into my personal language. The words I hear become connected to feelings, pictures and sounds associated with that conversation and other similar memories, so that I have a movie to play back for a particular conversation. However, when I play those movies in my mind, a part of me thinks everyone can see the same image, so I leave out certain aspects of that vision. This leads to people asking me questions when they try to figure out what I am talking about.

"You Don't Want to Go For a Ride"

When I remember, the objects, people, animals and emotions are very clear, but I don't see writing and I don't always have a clear memory of the words that were said. This led to some interesting fights with my husband when I was younger, because I could remember a scene where I had been upset with him, but I could not remember exactly what he had said. He would always want to know exactly what he had said and we would both become frustrated, because I remember being upset and he wanted to know how to behave so he wouldn't make me angry in the future. When I remember things, it can be very frustrating to see the books and papers in my memory and not be able to read the words, even though everything else in the memory is clear. It can be challenging to communicate and not become frustrated at the entire process.

My explanation is based on many years of experience and many mistakes when interacting with others. While I can't be sure of how John-John thinks or processes social situations, I suspect that he has built a similar set of scripts for his social interactions. His use of quotes and repetition of phrases that John and I use point to him following a limited set of rules, even when they aren't always appropriate.

Even writing this passage about my thought processes is at once interesting and frustrating, because I find myself wondering what I've left out. Fortunately, I have a good editor and beta readers to help decipher my thoughts and clarify them for the readers.

I have included references and resources for books I found helpful when my son was younger. It was very helpful to read how other families had reached out to their children and found a way to communicate. It also includes some additional resources that I have found since then.

Barron, Judy, Barron, Sean (1992): *There's a Boy in Here.* New York, New York. Simon & Schuster.

Grandin, Temple (1995): *Thinking in Pictures and Other Reports from My Life With Autism.* New York, New York. Doubleday.

Rimland, Bernard (1964). *Infantile Autism: The Syndrome and its Implications for a Neural Theory of Behavior.* New York, New York. Prentice Hall.

Stehli, Annabelle (1990): *The Sound of a Miracle.* New York, New York. Doubleday.

Higashida, Naoki (August 27, 2013): *The Reason I Jump: The Inner Voice of a Thirteen-Year-Old Boy with Autism.* New York, New York. Random House.

Robison, John Elder. (September 9, 2008): *Look Me in the Eye: My Life with Asperger's.* New York, New York. Three Rivers Press.

Silberman, Steve. (August 25, 2015): *NeuroTribes: The Legacy of Autism and the Future of Neurodiversity.* New York, New York. Avery/Penguin Random House.

Suskind, Ron.(April 1, 2014): *Life, Animated: A Story of Sidekicks, Heroes and Autism.* Glendale, California. Kingswell.

An alternative therapy for communicating with non-verbal autistic children – http://www.halo-soma.org/

Baby Sign Language. n.d. http://www.babysignlanguage.com/

Magro, Kerry. "These 21 Books Will Help You Learn More About Autism."*Kerry Magro*. N.d. http://kerrymagro.com/these-21-books-will-help-you-learn-more-about-autism/

7

The Education of J. T. –
Homeschooling

John

After moving back to San Diego, we continued to look for ways to help John-John. After our experience with the pre-school, we weren't too thrilled with our public education options. We had heard of a local place called the Autism Research Institute, where we received information and a confirmation of J.T.'s autism. From what we could tell about public school in the mid-'90s, there weren't many options for helping children with this condition.

We were now better off financially, but private school was still not affordable and we weren't sure we could find a place that would accept our son. We still didn't agree with the idea that we had to sit back and wait to put him into an institution. Tammy had been busy researching homeschooling and the legalities of setting up a curriculum. The setup for home school depends on the law in each state. In California, there were four options at the time. After many discussions, Tam and I decided to homeschool him. After reviewing our legal options, we decided to set up as a private school. That was the beginning of the Harpster Academy, with an enrollment of one student. Since I had established a better relationship with him than Tammy had at the time, we decided that I would stay home and teach him while Tam earned the living for the household.

Children did not have to be enrolled in school until they were six years old, so we had a little time to set up our system and figure out the paperwork. We worked with two organizations: the Home School Legal Defense Association (HSLDA) and the California Homeschool Network. Both groups provided guides and paperwork for the private school option, which was very helpful. I set up a file drawer for attendance records and Tammy filled out the paperwork for our little school. I also kept a notebook for tracking our studies and a log I filled out every year I homeschooled J.T. Since Tammy was listed as the principal for our school, she would fill out the registration paperwork each year after making sure she got the latest forms. I kept a record of the school hours for J.T. and we never had any problems with how we ran our academy.

Due to our uncertainty during the first couple of years, we looked for guidance regarding the curriculum for our son. For kindergarten, even though we did not have to set up our school yet, we decided to get some help in assessing J.T.'s needs. We found a place called the National Association for Child Development (NACD), which offered to evaluate and provide guidance for parents with their children. Other places offered similar training, but they were too expensive or didn't seem like they would help—or both. The NACD appealed to us because we liked their idea that parents should be involved with the child's education. We used their services for about a year, and we drove up to Utah a couple of times to have J.T. evaluated and bring new curricula home. They provided suggestions on subjects to go over with him and also provided materials. Some exercises didn't work so well, while others were very well-received. One such exercise involved J.T. listening to certain music to help him get used to certain sounds. When he listened to the CDs they provided, it would affect him emotionally and tears would stream down his face as he listened. However, he continued to listen to the music, in spite of how it appeared to affect him. We also performed regular schoolwork with flash cards.

When J.T. turned six, we set up our school formally. Tam continued her research and found a curriculum that she liked from a place called Oak Meadow. We ordered a copy, but the curriculum didn't fit our needs. The structured lessons, even at the kindergarten and first-grade level, were beyond what J.T. could comprehend. Because he had problems, he resisted the lessons or wouldn't respond when I tried to teach the information. The curriculum had a lot of flexibility and was of good quality, but it didn't fit our situation.

"You Don't Want to Go For a Ride"

In my experience teaching J.T., forcing him to learn topics did not work well. That approach works for many children regardless of whether they are interested in the subject matter, but it did not work for him. I remember very well trying to use this approach to teach him math. While reading, he experienced no problems and he maintained his enthusiasm. We were still working with the NACD. They had recommended using flash cards for math. and to have him sit down and learn simple addition and subtraction. He had progressed when I used flash cards for reading, but they did not work with math. I tried simple addition and subtraction cards, but meltdowns that had all but disappeared suddenly returned with a vengeance. This became a challenge, and I was bound and determined to teach him the concept, so I would force him to sit and look at the flash cards. He would try to run off and he screamed when I brought him back. I would get him and bring him back, while yelling that he needed to sit down. When I got out the flash cards, he would get up and run away again. I became very frustrated and this got old quickly, so I wound up putting locks on every door in the house so he couldn't get out while I tried to teach him.

We repeated this cycle of behavior every day while Tam was at work and it lasted for several weeks. One evening, while I vented to her about the home situation, we decided that it just wasn't worth trying to continue teaching him math. He had begun to resist learning other subjects, and he and I were both upset by the time evening rolled around. He had started to shut down and wanted to avoid all schooling, not just the math portion. I realized that I needed to be flexible and work with him instead of trying to force him into activities that he was learning to hate.

I dropped all lessons for a few days and gave J.T. a break from our routine. He eventually calmed down and I changed how we learned things, focusing on his interests instead of a set curriculum. This method is usually called unschooling and can be challenging to implement. It is based on the idea that children like to learn, and if they are allowed to focus on their own interests, they will learn quickly and discover other information related to that field. This method is very flexible and free–form, but it can lead to deficiencies in knowledge for children, since they aren't following a set curriculum and timetable for learning skills. However, the child does gain experience in how to learn and find information, which can be used to dig out data they need as they get older. In our case, this turned out to be the approach that J.T. could work with and which lowered the stress level in our home. Tam and I had enough stress in dealing with other aspects of J.T.'s behavior, and trying to force him to learn certain topics at a certain time didn't seem worth it.

Tam and I agreed that a child-centered learning process would work better for J.T. than setting up a curriculum and schedule. He and I spent many hours lying around the living room while researching and talking about whatever seemed to catch his interest at the time. If he wasn't interested in a subject, we just didn't talk about it. Over the years, he did show an interest in most things taught in schools. He simply covered them in the order he wanted, as his interest in each subject materialized. The last subject he learned was math–this as he realized how money was used. He learned math when he went to the store to pay for things out of his own allowance.

While Tam worked, I would lie on the couch with John-John and read stories. When he was younger, his favorite author was Dr. Seuss and he would read along with me. I used alphabet flash cards to teach him to read. He took to it really well and before I knew it, he was reading to me. At first, we bought big coffee table books with lots of pictures and he loved to look through them. As websites grew larger and contained more information, he would surf the Internet and get his information that way. He enjoyed many topics, including space travel, the interstate highway system, the Mars missions, commercial jetliners (he knows when and where every type of jet was built and its safety record) and computers (he learned to use the Internet early). When he became interested in a topic, he would read everything he could about that topic and look up references about other topics.

For example, one area of interest for him was plane crashes. He definitely enjoyed watching destruction of just about any sort, like other boys his age. As he grew older, he used the Internet to find information about major airline disasters in the U.S. Eventually, he researched information about different types of aircraft and which

161

airline used a particular model. He also liked to go to the airport and watch the planes land. When a particular aircraft prepared for takeoff, he would rattle off make, model, manufacturer, which airline used it and the other aircraft that the airline had used. While not always a practical skill, it did help him to learn about the world around him.

Space travel became another topic of interest. This started in 1996. When the news media ran constant stories about the Pathfinder mission to Mars, J.T. became fascinated with it and asked for information about it. He developed an interest in all things Mars, including its geography and NASA missions that had gone there. We hung a map of Mars on our dining room wall and J.T. memorized every location on the map, including where the missions had landed. He liked to go to the map, point to a location and name the mission that had landed at that spot or a named feature at that location. He would point to another area, name it and continue. Eventually he focused only on the Mars missions instead of the features. He knew the names of the missions, what they were to study and what information had been sent back.

Because of his research on the Mars missions, J.T. learned a lot about NASA and the space program. He even asked about the Challenger disaster and became interested in other spacecraft disasters around the world. He and I would find articles on the Internet about other space programs, and J.T. would look for information about each mission, when a spacecraft launched and which ones had crashed. We eventually discovered Wikipedia and I printed articles for us to read together. Since these pieces included links to other articles for the history of the country, J.T. would find them and we would read that information, too. I'm not sure how I stayed awake when we read Russian and Chinese history, but somehow I managed. In this way, starting with his interest in the Mars missions, he eventually became interested in learning US history and world history in order to better understand how the space programs got started.

One of his research projects involved the U.S. interstate road system. He learned about every highway, when it was built, which ones were still being built or planned for construction, what states they went through and how many miles they ran. We went on a trip to Wyoming in 2001 and he took pictures all along the route so he could have images of a highway he had read about. At least this skill had turned out somewhat useful before GPS units were commonplace. He always knew where we were and how to get to where we were going. This would annoy Tam a bit, because it turned J.T. into a backseat driver, but I always found it helpful to focus on my driving while he gave me directions. Even after we put a GPS in the car, his skill was still more useful and faster than trying to type an address or location into the module.

His memory is remarkable, much better than either of his parents. Besides the history of jets, history in general is another subject that he loves. He can name world events and when they happened. I just nod in agreement, since I have limited knowledge of history myself. He has continued learning about different subjects, including sports statistics for U.S. professional and college teams, science fiction universes such as Star Trek and Star Wars, and photography. He has never had much interest in advanced math, unlike Tam and myself, but he has learned enough math to understand how money works. He has also learned life skills such as laundry, basic cooking, yardwork and some very rudimentary cleaning. Because of the time I spent with J.T., I have come to the conclusion that children can learn things more quickly if they focus on their own interests.

Tamara

Before John-John became school-aged, I had already started looking at homeschooling, but I was prepared to put him in public school if John had strongly objected. I vividly remember my problems in school, and I didn't want my son to experience the teasing, and bullying that I had to endure. However, I still did not have enough confidence to speak up, and homeschooling was a fringe movement at the time – viewed as something practiced by hippies or Christian fundamentalists in order to keep their children away from "real" school. However, after our experience with the pre-school and comments from teachers looking forward to a chance to "practice" with our son with information from a class about autistic children, John also decided that homeschooling might work better for our family. I was also interested in Montessori academies, but we did not have the money at the time for a private learning center and there were waiting lists for those schools, anyway.

I had subscribed to some alternative parenting magazines and found several books with more information about homeschooling. I also read John Holt's books and felt that I had discovered a philosophy that agreed with how I thought children learned. I located a legal organization that would provide support to homeschooling families. We signed up when John-John was in first grade and became a private school – the Harpster Academy – in accordance with California law. During our early years, the public schools offered homeschooling options, but we had heard too many horror stories of parents who tried to work with their system. While academic instruction was important to us, our first focus was on reaching John-John and helping him to get along in this world. I felt we needed to build a foundation and a way to communicate or we were going to become very frustrated with trying to teach him reading, writing and arithmetic.

I still wanted him to be around other children, so I made attempts to find a group where he could simply play with kids his own age. I found one group that met for the sole purpose of getting the kids to socialize, but this didn't work well when John-John did not interact with the other children or respond when they tried to talk to him. I stopped going after a couple of visits due to worries about John-John's meltdowns and the lack of welcome from the other mothers. I still remember the looks directed my way when he acted out and how badly

I felt that my son didn't fit in. He acted too differently to be a part of the crowd and I did not have the social skills or confidence to try to overcome the stigma. I believe there are more groups now, including parents of autistic children, but homeschooling was too different at the time. There was not as much awareness of autism and the behaviors associated with it so parents and children were often viewed as bad people.

I was not as involved with the lessons during the early years, since I was usually tired by the end of the day and I did not have a lot of patience left for John-John. I did talk with my husband about our son's progress and I would research information for him if he needed it. With the increasing number of websites on the Internet, there was a lot more information available, but it could be extremely challenging to dig through it all. I kept my research skills sharp and followed the changing search technology as I continued to look for new data about autism, homeschooling and other topics as they came up.

I remember very well when my husband started teaching John-John math with the flash cards. We had bought a house in San Diego and everyone had settled in after our time apart the year before. John had to drive me to work every day so that John-John knew where I was, but in many other parts of our life things were much calmer. However, when the math lessons started, John-John began acting out in the evenings and John was usually angry by then because he was unable to work with John-John during the day. He did try to teach other things, but after a few weeks John-John spent most of the day trying to get away from the lessons. At some point, John decided to install locks on all of the doors and I agreed that it might help, both for the lesson plans and to keep John-John inside where he couldn't run away from the schooling. However, the meltdowns continued and got progressively worse. One night, while John and I were talking, I told him it wasn't worth it to try to force our son to learn math, especially since he had enjoyed the other lessons so much. I suggested that John take a break for a week or so to let John-John calm down. John did interrupt the schooling for a while, during which time he just spent time playing with John-John. Within a few days, everyone was so much calmer at our house. John reintroduced some of the lessons once things had settled down, but he stayed away from math for a long time. It wasn't until much later, when John-John started to comprehend money and what he could do with it, that he finally became interested in math.

John also had to keep our son in the house during school hours in order to avoid truancy reports. This was another reason John and I decided to put locks on the doors. An additional challenge revealed itself when we discovered that John-John did not fully understand the dangers of streets and other hazards in our neighborhood. I have read articles about autistic children wandering away from home, but at the time this was something we had to deal with on our own.

A major concern regarding autistic children is their tendency to wander away. Our decision about the locks may seem extreme, but after a couple of incidents, we felt they were necessary. One of the hardest aspects of raising John-John is in not being able to share some of these experiences because people might think we were bad, or worse, abusive parents. I have found in my research that other parents of autistic children have also taken steps to keep their child safe, such as using a leash, keeping doors locked and other security measures. However, these stories aren't often shared because the behavior is viewed as poor parenting instead of attempts to keep the child safe.[6] Both John and I decided that our child was not going to be featured on the six o'clock news because he had wandered off, so we took steps to prevent this behavior. When he was younger, we experienced two incidents of his wandering at the motel. In one instance, he had strolled out of the house, into the parking lot to the sidewalk right by the highway. This

---

[6] A study published in the *Pediatric* journal in 2012 showed that autistic children at the ages of four to seven are four times more likely to wander off than their unaffected siblings. Forty-nine percent of autistic children wander off and fifty three percent of those children were gone long enough to cause concern. From the ages of eight to eleven, autistic children are twenty-seven percent more likely to wander off than one percent of their unaffected siblings.

When autistic children wander, they leave their home, stores and classrooms. Close calls with traffic, and drowning are common. These children are less likely to respond to their name and have lower communication skills. These children went missing on average for forty-one minutes. The behavior was reported as one of the most stressful to deal with for parents of autistic children. The study was performed by researchers from the Interactive Autism Network and the Kennedy Krieger Institute. http://www.kennedykrieger.org/overview/news/nearly-half-children-autism-wander-or-%E2%80%9Cbolt%E2%80%9D-safe-places

occurred when he was two years old. The next time, we searched for him for thirty minutes while calling his name and looking through the house, motel rooms, garage and back yard. John and I were almost ready to call the police when I thought to check back in the bedroom, where I finally found him. He had fallen asleep on the floor behind the bed where I couldn't see him. While he had not strayed away from the house, his ability to hide frightened us. We realized that since he liked to run off whenever he could, he might go places where we could not keep an eye on him all of the time.

In the house we bought in San Diego, we lived on a very busy street and were worried about him running into traffic. I remember a story from that time about an autistic boy who had left his house. The parents called the police and conducted a search, but had no luck in the immediate neighborhood. Fortunately, their son was found within a few hours. He had crossed several busy roads and ended up at their favorite grocery store nearly four miles away! They found him standing near the chicken rotisserie, watching the birds turn round and round. He was simply fascinated by the rotating motion of the chickens.

Another time, in our neighborhood, a helicopter with a PA system flew near the house. The man on the bullhorn asked people to watch for an autistic girl who had wandered off while her parents were shopping. This happened just down the street from us, at a small shopping center. I never heard if they found her, but I remember thinking, "That could have been *my* son!"

Wandering was not the only behavior issue we had to deal with. At the age of five, J.T. responded better to direction, but if he experienced problems with performing a certain task, he would have a meltdown. Most people picture a meltdown as something that children go through for only a few minutes. They fight, kick, scream and carry on, and then it eventually stops when they realize that they aren't going to get their way.

John-John didn't stop the meltdowns—he kept them going and they sometimes escalated. If we tried to make him do something, he would fight us, lash out at us, try to hurt himself or us, or even break things. Locking him in a room by himself only made things worse. He would beat on the door incessantly until we let him out. He might take a break from the behavior for a few minutes, but once he had recharged his batteries, he would start acting out all over again.

As I had discovered when he was younger, regular discipline such as time-outs, spankings and yelling did not work. John never spanked him, but when he tried yelling or time-outs, John-John would still fight and lash out. John and I had to find creative ways to keep him and us safe, while at the same time trying to teach him some life skills. By locking him in the house, he could still bang into things, but it seemed to help that he knew that one of us was there with him and that he wasn't left alone.

When he was younger, we would sit next to him and talk quietly to him, try to reassure him while he screamed himself out. As he got older, we would move away from him during his meltdowns in order to avoid being struck while he worked through his anger. Most of the time, we did our best to not react strongly, yell or get angry with him, but there were times when John or I would lose our temper and add to the disruption. Ignoring him seemed to be most helpful in reducing his intensity level. We did have to occasionally repair a hole in the wall or door after a particularly intense meltdown, but at least he never injured himself or us enough to require medical attention.

As a result, we put extra locks on all the doors of the house and the gates on the fence outside. We were very thankful that John-John had not figured out how to climb fences. Otherwise, I'm not sure what we could have done to keep him in. You can tell regular children to stay inside the house and if they disobey you they get a time-out, yell at them or possibly even spanked them and they may learn after a couple of times. That didn't happen with John-John and we weren't even sure if he fully understood what we were trying to tell him.

He showed no fear and would only learn if he was injured in the process. For example, shortly after we moved back to San Diego, he once tried to be friendly with a dog next door, but the dog bit him. As he grew older, he became more responsive when we told him to do something, but when he was between four and eight years old, we had to be harsh in order to keep him from doing things that were too dangerous. We also stayed home as a family more often because we didn't want him to act up in public. People nowadays seem to be more understanding of autistic behavior such as meltdowns, but at the time, people around us just shot us dirty looks for not "controlling our child." I felt ashamed of his behavior and it became easier to just stay home or find isolated areas where he could run around and not be noticed, like the zoo. I always looked for escape routes, so I could take him away quickly if there was ever a problem. When he was smaller, that approach was easier because I could tuck him under my arm and walk out. However, as he grew older, it became more difficult to deal with him. We gradually went out less as a family, due to the stress of trying to keep him quiet and under control.

As for his education, John experienced success with his teaching methods. John-John would focus on the topics that interested him and absorb as much information as he could. He also continued to draw and he began to branch out with his imagery. He wouldn't draw just one or two pictures. He would draw stories and go through reams of paper. We shopped at big-box stores or an office supply and buy a case of copy paper every other month or so. Once an idea popped into his head, he would use a lot of paper to draw about it and capture every detail. As he gained vocabulary, he would tell us his story about the picture and describe what happened. When he couldn't think of the right word, he pointed to the picture and that would prompt us to give him what he needed. As a result, J.T. found another path for communicating with us.

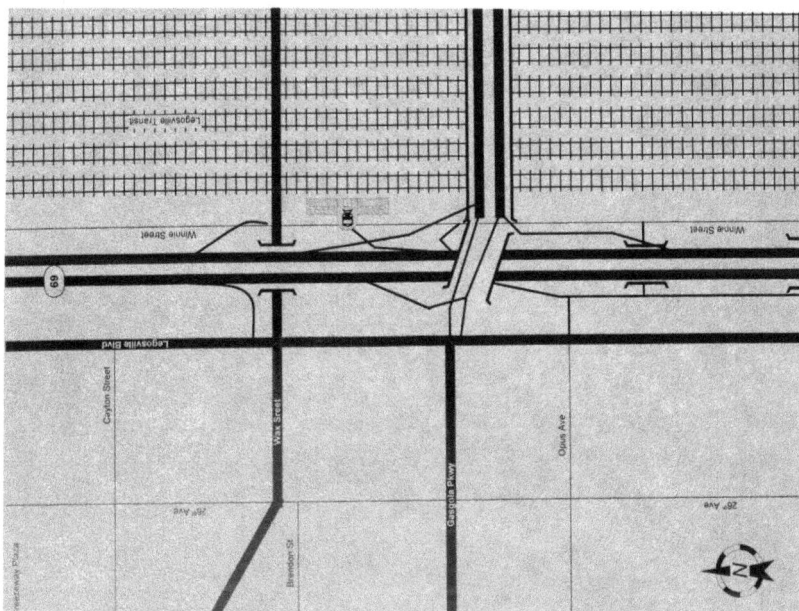

Figure 20 – Map of Legosville, Drawn by John-John

Figure 21 – Logo Created by John-John for Legosville Mass Transit

Figure 22 – The Flag of Mexilego

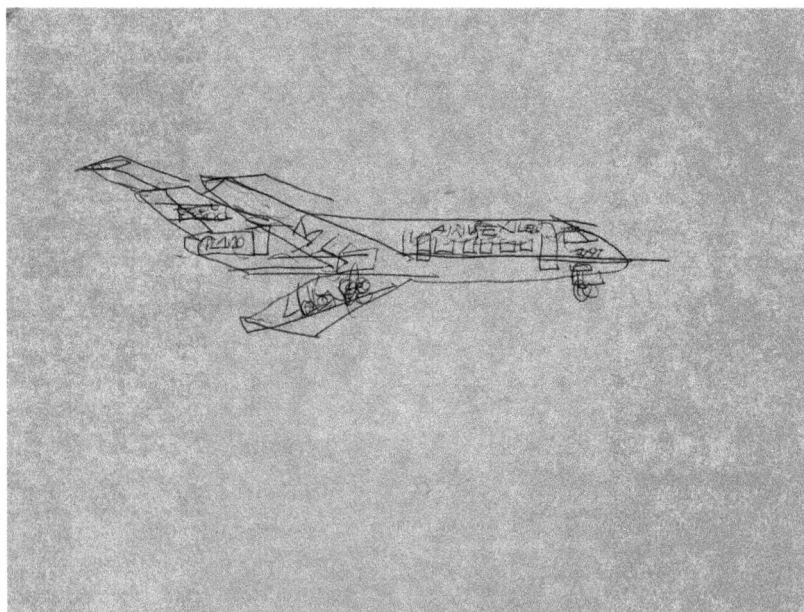

Figure 23 – Drawing of an Airplane for Mexilego Airlines

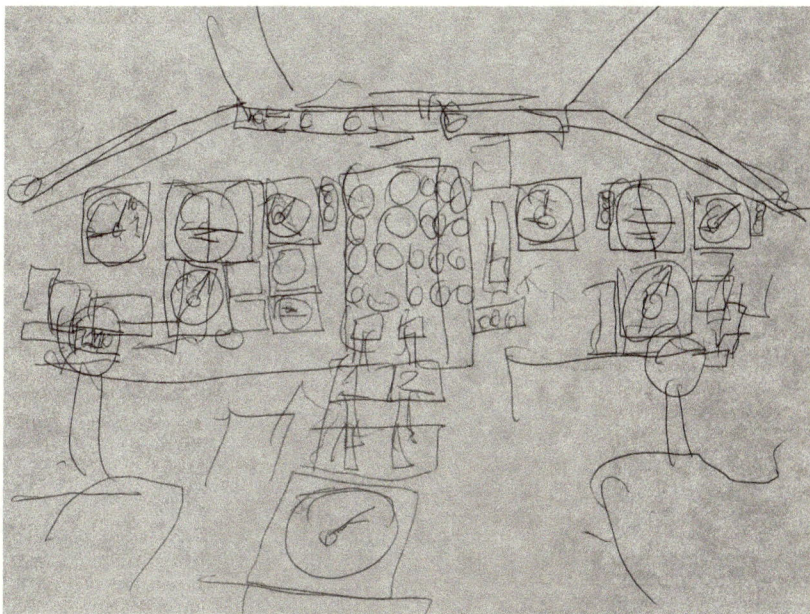

Figure 24 –Cockpit of an Airplane John-John Researched

Figure 25 – Front View of a Jet with Landing Gear Down

Figure 26 – Concept Art for Bricksville.net Website Logo

Figure 27 – Digital Drawing of Bricksville.net Logo: One by Me, the Final by John-John

Figure 28 – Close-Up Map Detail for Legosville

Figure 29 – Concept Poster for *CyborgMan* Movie

John M. Harpster & Tamara Harpster

Resources, References, and Reflections –
Homeschooling Resources

John and I both strongly felt that our son needed more attention from us, so we changed to a situation that supported our family. Homeschooling was the best option for us. For others, public or private school may be a better option. For parents who are interested in homeschooling, I have listed some resources I used in years past, as well as some more recent ones. Some public school districts offer homeschooling as an option. In these cases, the schools provide curricula and lessons for the parents to use. In some cases, the child can join in classroom activities and take advantage of some of the positive aspects of socialization that might be available.

Over the years, I have gone back and forth on our decision to homeschool and whether it was the right choice. I mostly feel that it was the right one, because he now seems comfortable with going out by himself, he continues to learn new things and he is interested in the world. I have heard from other parents of young autistic adults about how their son or daughter does not want to leave the house or try new things because of poor experiences, such as bullying or lack of adequate educational supports in traditional schooling. However, I also wonder if my son might have been a little more flexible if he had to deal with teachers and other children away from us. I know that my childhood was very difficult and I have no desire to repeat many parts of it, but I did learn skills because of the hardships I endured.

I think it is important to help the child and the family find a balance that supports everyone's needs in what is often a chaotic situation. I don't think there is one solution that will work for every family, simply because not every autistic child is exactly alike. This section offers alternatives for families that are dissatisfied with their own children's school situations.

Autism Web: A Parent's Guide to Autism Spectrum Disorder.
www.autismweb.com.

"Being Free: Why We Choose to Homeschool Our Autistic Son."
Respectfully Connected. April 4, 2015.
http://respectfullyconnected.blogspot.com.au/2015/04/being-free-why-we-choose-to-homeschool.html

National Association for Child Development (NACD).[7]
http://www.nacd.org/.

Holt, John. (1964, revised 1982) How Children Fail. New York, Merloyd Lawrence, Delta/Seymour Lawrence.

Holt, John. (1967, revised 1983) How Children Learn. New York, Merloyd Lawrence, Delta/Seymour Lawrence.

Holt, John. (1989) Learning All the Time. New York, Merloyd Lawrence, Delta/Seymour Lawrence.

Homeschooling Autism. http://homeschoolingautism.blogspot.com/

---

[7] This organization assesses the child and works with the parents on the recommended curriculum. The study plan is unique and designed specifically for each individual child.

John M. Harpster & Tamara Harpster

Homeschooling Autism Resources. A2Z Home's Cool – Alphabet of Homeschooling.
http://a2zhomeschooling.com/concerns_homeschooling/homeschooling_au tistic_children/

8

Living with Autism

John

Tammy has told me that she thinks she is autistic, too. I very rarely see that in her, but sometimes I know what she's referring to. For instance, sometimes J.T. walks up to me and asks, "When?" Nothing preceded the question and sometimes I had not spoken to him since the previous day. He would just ask, "When?" We must have had a conversation in his head, but I would have no idea what he was talking about.

Tammy does the same thing. Sometimes she walks up to me and asks, "Why?" I would search my mind frantically to try to remember if I had wronged her in some way, but it was never about that–simply that we were having a conversation in her head that I wasn't privy to and now it was time for me to explain myself. I have wasted many precious hours trying to explain to both of them that complete sentences have both a subject and a predicate. They are not just one-word inquiries.

In addition, both she and J.T. have rules they need me to follow in order to keep their stress levels down. Most of the time, their rules aren't in conflict, but when they are, it can be quite lively at home. Several times, I have had to step in to calm things down, especially when J.T. was younger.

John Thomas had been quite a handful as a youngster. This plus the fact that no one at the time really knew what caused autism helped me to come to the conclusion that we had had enough children. I think Tamara wanted one more, but I also thought the condition might be genetic, so I wasn't taking any chances. I finally won that discussion, so J.T. was the only child we ever had.

As he got older, his earlier behavior of running in the house and humming expanded. The house wasn't big enough for him so he would run around the yard while stomping his feet and humming. He would repeat this behavior for minutes at a time, running and humming for reasons we could not understand. I now know that this behavior is called "stimming," which is short for self-stimulation and cannot truly be understood without seeing it in action. In J.T.'s case, it can be quite dizzying if watched for very long. When he was younger, it helped him to run off his excess energy. As a result, he slept better at night. However, once he was up, he was one big ball of activity pretty much all day long. This behavior had been less noticeable in his early years and seemed closer to the normal activity level of a toddler or preschooler. He would run back and forth in the house during the day, but the behavior would not last as long.

We continued to live in the San Diego area while Tam worked, and during this time, J.T.'s enthusiasm for learning peaked. He and I spent hours every day reading about subjects that piqued his interest. As described in the previous chapter, when J.T. was six, we started homeschooling. However, the year before that, he began picking up more language. He even worked on his language skills in a different way: he repeated his words over and over. As I drove down the street, J.T. would see a stop sign and say, "stop sign." Then he would repeat the phrase four or five times. He didn't use the words to communicate. He just kept repeating them. But we noticed that he had begun talking more. He also seemed to understand more of what we said and all of us were a little less frustrated as a result.

He also became fully potty-trained by age five. We saw signs that he knew what he needed to do. He just showed no interest in doing it. The first thing we realized is that he stayed dry at night and didn't need a diaper. However, he still had problems during the day. Tam's mom came to visit for his fifth birthday and talked to him about using the toilet. J.T. and his Nana have always gotten along well and they have a bond, in spite of not seeing each other very often. A week or two after her visit, I tried again to get him to use the toilet. That very day, he used it for the first time and only had one or two accidents after that.

This was a big change and it helped to encourage us that he could grow out of some of his behaviors.

He continued to draw, but now he used paper and pen in addition to his computer drawings. He drew his stories and showed them to us while telling the story using the words he had learned as we practiced our lessons. We realized that the drawings helped him to communicate ideas and learn vocabulary. At first, the drawings were just a tool to help J.T. communicate, but I eventually used them to show him how to interact with other people as well. I would draw several sheets of stick figures and word balloons to show how a conversation might go. Then I showed them to J.T. and asked him what he or the other person might say. He liked to draw and he was also interested in the stick figures. He liked to repeat them and he quickly picked up on how to answer another person in typical conversation, such as saying "hi" to a friend or neighbor.

As his communication skills sharpened, the intensity of his meltdowns gradually decreased. Instead of dropping to the floor to flail and scream, he would simply stomp his feet and run around the house. We worked with him to keep him from hitting and running into things when he acted out of control, but sometimes there was a lot of anger and irritation to express. As we all found ways to communicate with each other, the anger incidents decreased in frequency.

We also spent time together as a family. One activity we especially enjoyed was to watch television and a favorite program was *Rescue 911* with William Shatner. J.T. loved that show, and Tammy and I would sit with him every night to watch the reruns. It ran for at least a couple of years after we moved back to San Diego. Most of the time, J.T. didn't like to sit still for TV, but he would watch this show with us. He eventually lost interest, but it was good quality family time for all of us while it lasted.

Tamara

During John-John's early years, I wanted to have another child. However, after the challenges we experienced during his toddler and pre-school years, I slowly let go of that desire. When I became aware of my depression and how it affected my family, I realized that I did not want a recurrence of postpartum depression. Likewise, a strong possibility existed that we might have another autistic child. All factors considered I eventually gave up on my notion of an ideal family with a boy and a girl. I still sometimes wish we had decided to have another child, so John-John could have a sibling, but it was just too risky and there were so many other challenges to overcome. John and I also felt that it would not have been fair to the other child to bring him or her into this scenario.

We developed coping strategies for our family in the early years. I previously mentioned how we kept everything locked down, but that wasn't the only area where we differed from other parents. Before John-John, we were used to driving around, going out to eat, seeing movies and doing other things as a couple. In J.T.'s first year, we would hire a babysitter, but as he got older and acted out more often, we no longer felt comfortable leaving him with anyone. Once he got really wound up or angry, he was hard to handle and we simply didn't want to explain to a sitter about how he might act–or deal with the phone calls as they tried to control him and his difficult behavior.

When he was younger, we would go out to eat as a family, but between the ages of five and twelve, this became more difficult. John-John only liked certain foods, he wouldn't sit still at the table and he didn't want to stay very long. Children without autism also act out in public, but most of them don't scream at the top of their lungs, hit their parents or the table, or leap from their chairs and run back and forth while humming in order to deal with their situation. Since I am very uncomfortable with appearing different in front of others and because of the difficulty of trying to control John-John in these situations, John and I began staying home more often and didn't spend much time just as a couple. Since we are both introverts, this wasn't too much of a hardship, but there were times when we would have liked to go out by ourselves.

John and I had chosen to live far away from both of our families, and neither of us is very good at meeting people and making new friends. This meant that we didn't know many people to spend time with or who could help us. John did befriend a neighbor down the street who was all right with how John-John behaved, so John and his new acquaintance would meet during the day while I worked. John stayed home to take care of our son while I made friends on the job. I even went out to lunch with them to take a break from the stresses of home life. Between the two of us, we had some semblance of a social life, just not a large network of friends.

When I finally admitted that I suffered from depression, I started taking medication for it. This was a crucial step in helping me cope with my situation. After many years of mental and emotional pain, I finally began to find a way to be more comfortable with myself. This helped to reduce the number of tense encounters with my son and I eventually got along with him a little more easily. I also found it easier to deal with stressful situations at work, which helped to reduce my depression as well.

On weekends, I would take John-John to the zoo or out for a drive to give my husband a break. For many years, we had an unwritten rule: During non-work hours, neither John nor I would leave the other with John-John for more than two hours at a time. Due to the stress of dealing with his outbursts, leaving one person at home with him for longer than 2-3 hours was too much, so we established a routine. One of us would take a break for two hours while the other watched John-John. We occasionally ventured out into public together as a family, but this didn't happen very often because of others' disapproval of John-John's behavior.

I also remember about John-John's fussy eating. I have read about how diet can help reduce autistic symptoms, but with all the battles we endured, John and I decided to let this one go. I recall the childhood battles I had with my own parents about eating. I did not want to repeat that with John-John. After I left home, the issues with my food choices were not resolved until my mid-thirties and I wanted John-John to avoid some of the anxiety that could be associated with forced eating. We did not have family-type meals where we all sat at the dinner table and J.T. ate a lot of fast food. Eventually, my husband established a first-name basis with the employee at the drive-through window.

Even small changes in John-John's food and how it was served could cause problems. For example, he required a straw for any drink we brought home for him. It was not acceptable to pour the drink into another glass. There had to be a straw. Otherwise, he would have a meltdown. We started to keep them in the house in case the straw from the restaurant didn't make it home, but even that didn't work all the time. I once forgot the straw and didn't make sure that they put one in the bag. When we gave him his drink, he looked through the bag and noticed the absence. "Where's straw?" he inquired.

I answered, "I forgot, Can't you just drink it out of the cup?"

"Need straw!" he yelled back.

"Sorry, I forgot," I replied. "Let me see if there are any in the cupboard." I looked through the shelves in vain—no straw.

"Need straw!" he yelled again, only now he had begun running up and down the hallway, humming loudly and beating his hands against the walls.

"I can't find one–calm down!" I yelled. But by then, he had gone into meltdown mode. He would "stim" for the next twenty minutes or so, running back and forth, humming and occasionally beating his hands against the walls. Sometimes he would come over and try to hit me while I protected myself–all the while trying not to hurt him. This upset me greatly, to the point that I had to walk away from the situation while he ran himself out. He eventually calmed down, but it was really hard on both of us. Because we had such problems with this aspect of his meltdowns, I still become anxious about making sure we bring him a straw when we pick up his food. My anxiety about having everything prepared just so carries into other situations as well, although he has developed more coping skills dealing with unexpected events.

We also experienced problems involving J.T.'s experiments with chemicals around the house, especially in my workshop. He went through a period where he liked to get various bottles from around the house and mix their contents. We had either locked up most things or disposed of them, so most of the time his experimentation was limited to dumping the dish soap into the sink and running water to see how many bubbles he could generate. I had a workshop set up where I kept supplies for my hobbies and crafts. This included acrylic paints and wood stain, along with paint brushes and rags that I would use to apply the paint or stain. He didn't drink or eat anything volatile, but he did like to play with my paints and rearrange my belongings. I remember coming home one time to find out he had used up most of my black acrylic paint to cover various items in my workshop.

He also developed a fascination with fire, which many children seem to like, so it seemed like a somewhat normal behavior. I occasionally burned candles and incense in my workshop while I worked on my projects. John-John figured out how to use matches to light my candles and burn things with them. I went out to my shop one day after I got home from work to find a layer of ash on everything and some partially burned paper near the mess. I would also find wax poured into items. I would have to clean out my work area, clean out the wax from items where it had been dropped and clean my tools before using them.

From my experiences growing up, I remembered my own fascination with fire. But I had an outlet: on Girl Scout camping trips, I could build fires and play with them, but because of John-John's problems with people, he did not have access to this same outlet. Because of this, his fascination with fire could be quite scary at times. I remember an incident during my childhood of a fire started by children in the area. The police brought them home, no one was hurt and no property was damaged, so the children were warned and they learned to not do that again. However, John-John seemed compelled to keep experimenting, even though he did not yet fully understand what could happen if the blaze burned out of control. I would come home and find black ash coating everything in my workshop, I would clean things up, do some work and tell him that he shouldn't burn things, that it could be dangerous. Many weeks would go by and again I would find ash covering everything in my workshop. I told him again to not burn things in my workshop, but it took a few more repetitions before he moved onto other things.

He also liked to turn on the gas stove to see what could burn or blacken in the flames. Even though it only happened a couple of times, John and I scolded J.T. about the dangers of burning things in the house. Another time, he decided to see what would happen if he put various items in the microwave. Fortunately the aluminum foil did not cause a fire, but I never could quite get rid of all the black smudges that collected inside that appliance. On the one hand, I was glad that he was experimenting with things in his environment, but on the other hand I also worried about him hurting himself or others when he played with fire. I remember watching the old *Emergency 911* show; I think almost every episode had a story about children who played with fire and severely burned themselves.

I was amazed at how fast J.T. could move when I blew up after discovering another of his experiments. At least he didn't giggle as much as he had when he was younger. I believe his fire-starting behavior finally stopped when we caught him lighting one in the back yard. At least he took safety precautions this time. He had placed the paper in the barbecue grill and the water hose was at the ready, but it wasn't much fun to smell smoke and realize it was coming from our own property. John and I really blew up and our son actually looked contrite this time instead of giggling and running off. I don't remember how long this behavior went on. I think it was off and on for a year or so. John and I were both relieved as time went on and we stopped finding any more evidence of him playing with fire around the house.

Since he finally figured that fires were not a good idea, John-John became fascinated with dry ice. He liked to seal dry ice into containers so he could watch them burst open in our back yard, and he giggled in delight as they exploded. John and I happily supported this activity. The plastic containers burst open but did not break and he stayed in our back yard during these experiments. At the time, I was just happy he wasn't trying to burn things anymore. A few years later, when dry ice bombs were left at some schools, I was even happier that he had moved beyond that stage in his life. Amazingly, neither the police nor the fire department ever came to visit our home, in spite of our son's interest in fire.

At times, he could be quite helpful by noticing things we missed. John-John once called out to me that there was a fire behind our house, so naturally I thought the worst. However, when I looked out the window, I realized that he hadn't started this one. Instead, some neighborhood kids had set some abandoned furniture ablaze in the alley behind us. I called 911 while a neighbor across the way doused the scorched sofa with water until the fire department arrived. Another time, John-John came to tell me that the doggy was gone. Somehow our dog had found a way to get out of the yard, so I had to chase after her. This happened several times before we fixed the hole in the fence, and each time he would run in to tell us about the dog leaving the yard. He would become very anxious and we had to drop everything to go find her, or he would start another meltdown as he worried about her being hit in traffic.

I also recognized J.T.'s sense of humor. I took a series of pictures of him one day when he decided that he needed to put on every pair of his underwear he owned. I think he must have had on about 20 pairs at once under a pair of shorts. I grabbed my camera and took several shots as he posed for me, grinning each time. I still like to look at them and smile at his silliness. Another time, I came home from work and went to the back yard before dinner to check on some project or plants I was working on. John-John was already back there, playing in the dirt and water so by then he was pretty muddy. Right after I came out the back door, he walked up to me with his hand stuck out to shake mine. As I grabbed it, he said, "Hello there, good to meet you–I'm filthy." It caught me off guard and I laughed so hard that tears streamed down my face as he grinned at me. It was one of those moments where I felt more like a normal mom with a normal child who was just being silly.

While there were lighter moments, more traditional activities such as holidays were difficult for us. I eventually gave up many of the traditions I had grown up with because they just caused too much stress in our house. Christmas, however, didn't cause too much stress. If we hid the presents before Christmas day and brought them out on Christmas morning, John-John wasn't too concerned and enjoyed all of the gifts he received. Our only problem at Christmas before John-John turned five was his interest in pulling every ornament within his reach from the tree. Every year I took pictures of our Christmas tree and each succeeding year's images show the ornaments higher and higher on the tree. When he turned five, the last picture showed about a foot of decorations at the top of the six-foot tree. Fortunately, by the time he was six, he had decided that the ornaments could stay up, so we were finally able to decorate normally.

For many years, I was disappointed when Halloween rolled around and he would express no interest in going trick-or-treating. I think I took him out one or two years when he was pre-school age, but it added stress in trying to get him to wear a costume that he had no interest in. He also showed no interest in getting the candy, so I sadly let go of the idea of taking him trick-or-treating. Then, when he was around ten or eleven, he somehow realized that he could get free candy—but only on that night. He continued with the new-found tradition well into his teens. He was a big kid, but I didn't worry about it because he had missed so many years. This was yet another time I felt more like a normal parent, although John-John didn't show much interest in choosing his costume for several years. However, once he figured out that he could get free candy, he definitely looked forward to Halloween. He also seemed to understand that he couldn't go trick-or-treating every night, and I don't remember any meltdowns or frustration associated with it. When he did indicate an interest in the costumes, he picked things like Uncle Sam and LEGO Man. He also dressed up as Harry Potter one year, complete with wand and glasses. Sadly, he was disappointed when he tried to use the wand and no magic occurred. I was disappointed myself. I wouldn't have minded visiting the Hogwarts School of Witchcraft and Wizardry, even if I couldn't attend as a student.

The last time he went out, at age sixteen, we did hear a few negative comments about how he was too big for it, but most people were okay with the big kid dressed as LEGO Man going from house to house for candy like all the other children. Since he was fully grown at 6'2", he made for a very large trick-or-treater.

We never held an Easter egg hunt, and he never experienced the agony and the ecstasy of exchanging hearts for Valentine's Day. At Thanksgiving, we sat as a family for a few minutes while he ate a few bits of his food before he left the table. He did enjoy the fireworks on Independence Day, but only from a distance, due to the noise and the crowds. Since I also don't like large groups, we always watched the fireworks from a distance. This meant that we were never close enough for the noise to really bother him. His Nana always sent him cards for all the holidays and he seemed to like them—especially as he got older and understood the value of the money inside.

Our life went on, we all got older and things didn't remain the same. I see now that we endured more than our share of stress, but we made time for fun every now and then. It can be all too easy to focus on the negative, but there were many episodes when we truly enjoyed each other.

Resources, References and Reflections – Living with Autism

Due to the issues of raising an autistic child, the stress can take a heavy toll on one or both of the parents. Depression can occur and parents may divorce because one partner feels unable to handle the stress. If siblings are involved, they may resent the autistic child due to the extra attention, or they may develop coping mechanisms to stay in the background and out of the way, due to the chaos created in the household. Based on our experiences, we feel it is important for caregivers to make time for themselves and not feel ashamed to ask for help. The analogy of "putting on the parent's oxygen mask before the child's" is a good one to remember. If you aren't getting the emotional oxygen you need, you won't be able to help your child as well as you can. The following are resources for coping with depression and tools for the mental well-being for the families of autistic children.

Brown, Bene. "The Power of Vulnerability." *Ted Talk.* June 2010. September 29, 2015. http://www.ted.com/talks/brene_brown_on_vulnerability.

Firneno, Jack. "What they don't talk about: One family's life with three children on the autism spectrum." *The Wire.* August 6, 2014. September 29, 2015. http://midweekwire.com/2014/08/06/what-they-dont-talk-about/

Frank, a.k.a. Autism Daddy. *Autism Daddy Blog.* http://www.autism-daddy.blogspot.com/.

Kim, Cynthia. "The Importance of Past on the Left. *Musings of an Aspie.* January 5, 2013. September 29, 2015. http://musingsofanaspie.com/2013/01/05/the-importance-of-the-pasta-on-the-left/

Lee, Briannon. "Loving You to the Outside of Outer Space ..." *Respectfully Connected: Journeys in Parenting and Neurodivergence.* July 17, 2015. September 29, 2015. http://respectfullyconnected.blogspot.com.au/2015/07/loving-you-to-outside-of-outer-space.html

"Managing Behavioral Difficulties in ASD Children." *Durham Region Autism Services.* Viewed on September 29, 2015.

Margolis, Rachel. "Parental Well-Being Surrounding First Birth as a Determinant of Further Parity Progression." *Springer Link.* August 4, 2015. September 29, 2015. http://link.springer.com/article/10.1007/s13524-015-0413-2.

Menelly. "Blogspam and Information by Adult Autistics for Parents of Newly Diagnosed Kids." *Reddit.com.* November 10, 2014. September 29, 2015. https://www.reddit.com/r/autism/comments/2lv6k7/blogspam_and_information_by_adult_autistics_for/.

Mitchell, David. "David Mitchell. Learning to Live With My Son's Autism." *The Guardian.* June 29, 2013. September 29, 2015.

John M. Harpster & Tamara Harpster

http://www.theguardian.com/society/2013/jun/29/david-mitchell-my-sons-autism

Szalavitz, Maia. "The Boy Whose Brain Could Unlock Autism." *Medium.com.* December 11, 2013. https://medium.com/matter/the-boy-whose-brain-could-unlock-autism-70c3d64ff221

9

More Roads to Communication: LEGO Bricks and the Swamp

John

As the '90s passed, our family continued to adjust to life in the big city. Autism doesn't stop anyone from getting older and J.T. continued to grow up. In some ways, he seemed like a normal boy. He showed interests in things that crashed, occasional humor and typical childish behavior. On the flip side, we could see that he was just not like other children. He would run around in our back yard and hum for very long periods of time. He only liked certain foods—and heaven help us if it wasn't prepared correctly. Chicken sandwiches brought from the McDonald's down the street could never have had lettuce or tomato on them, and picking the vegetables off the sandwich was not good enough. We had to take the sandwich back and get a fresh one or he would have nothing to do with it. Once I got into the car and pretended to go back to McDonald's while I really just went around the block, stopped to take the lettuce and tomatoes off the sandwich, and drove back home. That one time is the only instance I remember fooling him about the sandwiches. It was a bad day for us when McDonald's changed from the round bun with no sesame seeds to a long bun with sesame seeds. The first few times I asked for a round bun, the chicken stuck out because it was now shaped for the new buns. J.T. finally accepted that McDonald's wasn't going to change back, but it was not an enjoyable transition for us.

In some ways, J.T. was ahead of his peers in his knowledge of the world. He followed the news—especially current events—and looked up many articles on Wikipedia. Once he became interested in a subject, he would learn everything he could about it. If the topic didn't grab his attention, he would fight—literally kicking and screaming—against being told anything about it. As his vocabulary gradually increased, he shared the new information with us. However, whenever we tried to have a conversation with him, we didn't have much luck. Any back-and-forth dialogue would give way to a monologue of recited facts. He spoke to us, but it had to be done his way, when he was ready.

At other times, he behaved like a normal child. He had a very active imagination and especially enjoyed playing with his toys. Tam's mother had bought him a wooden train set, with which he would busy himself by setting up the railroad and running the engine and cars around the tracks. He also liked ramming his toy cars into the train set and watching them crash into each other. During this play time, we could hear him talking about what was happening, just nothing intelligible. He did eventually start using words that we understood, but he would also hum at times as he moved the toys around. Tam would help him build his train set at times, but he mostly played by himself and didn't seem too interested in receiving any help. He was the only grandchild on both sides of the family for many years and because of this he had many toys. He enjoyed spreading them out in the patio room, which was fine because we were just happy that we weren't tripping over them in the main part of the house.

Where his creativity truly came into play was outdoors. He loved to play in water and mud, and a plastic wading pool sometimes wasn't enough. However, this was hard on our house and yard. The house we bought in San Diego was in good shape when we first moved in. The yard was well-maintained and the property looked nice. An older couple owned it before us and had kept up the yard and the interior. The place was spotless, so it was a cozy little home for our small family. We didn't have to work to keep the house up at first, but the longer we lived there, the harder it became to keep up with maintenance. As J.T. grew older and began investigating, we protected things and locked them away in an attempt to keep him out of trouble and the house in decent shape. Our primary focus was to help him communicate and find a place in the world, so house maintenance gradually took a back seat if it interfered with his communication or staying calm around the house.

One of the areas that changed, and not always for the better, was the back yard. Over several years, one part of our yard became his little playground. He mixed water with dirt to create mud buildings, roads and small lakes. At first the area was small, only a few feet in length and width. This area gradually increased to the point where we began to call it his "swamp." The space took up about a quarter of the back yard, a mixture of dirt, sand, mud, rocks and water that he spent a lot of time reshaping. He also used toy cars, trucks, people and sometimes buildings in his pretend play. He would move the dirt and mud around to create lakes and rivers, and then shaped the mud into buildings.

When he got older, he used a shovel to dig a hole for more water. Over time, he dug an area that was deep enough for wading. Fortunately, even though dry periods are commonplace in Southern California, there wasn't a shortage at that time, so he would run water into the area on a regular basis. This kept the water fresh and the bill was definitely worth the money, since it kept him busy during the day. This experience nurtured his imagination, so we just left him to his devices. However, that eventually made for some real work. In his teens, he finally outgrew the swamp, the water dried up and he moved some dirt back into the area he had dug. However, grass still didn't grow there and it was very uneven. When we finally put the house on the market, we all had to take turns raking and re-seeding to return the area to its original condition. The grass in the area was not as green as when we first moved in, but it looked much better than the mud and water that had been there for so many years.

Fortunately, he was willing to take baths at night, because he was just filthy after playing in the "swamp" all day. This was not necessarily a peculiarity, for our son showed no interest in showers, I suspect, because of an incident when he was a toddler. When he tried to shower, he slipped and fell. After more than ten years, he still wouldn't stand under a shower. He just ran away and hollered at the top of his lungs if we tried to get him to take one. But he sure did love his baths.

When J.T. was ten or so, he got his first set of LEGO bricks, but he wasn't very interested at first. Tam helped him put them together, but he didn't show any desire to put them together himself. During the Christmas season, when he was nearly twelve, this changed in a big way. He started a project that lasted for the next several years. He set up a portable table in the living room and built a small city on it with his LEGO bricks. For Christmas, we had bought some extra decorations, including cotton with glitter on it. We put the cotton under the tree with some small houses to make a Christmas scene. When he saw this, he decided the cotton and glitter would look better in his little town and moved everything to the table that held his LEGO village. He had also learned to use a camera and he took many pictures of his town for Christmas. We had just bought a brand-new digital camera, which was state-of-the-art technology for the time. He learned how to use the camera and was allowed to use it so long as he was careful with it.

His LEGO village remained for about a week before an imaginary fire struck and destroyed the city. J.T. moved the cotton around and reshaped it so it looked like smoke, then he knocked over the LEGO buildings as they "burned." He took pictures of the destruction and was very excited to show us what had happened to the town. I remember finding glitter all around the house for months after he had destroyed that tiny village. We would clean the house and think we had gotten all of the glitter this time, then find a new pocket of it about a month later. When we moved a few years ago, we still found some glitter from that Christmas that had occurred ten years earlier.

The Christmas season came and went, but the folding table with the city remained. After another week had passed, he decided to rebuild the town. We were glad he had become so creative, but we soon decided that we wanted our living room back. In January, Tam and I carefully moved Legosville to the large patio room in the back of the house. After the town was situated in its new home, J.T. thought that the room just looked too empty. Over the next few years, we added more tables and LEGO bricks, so his creation just grew and grew.

J.T. continued to take pictures with the digital camera. We both saw that it helped him make sense of the world around him. J.T. used the pictures to tell us stories about the town, the people and the street names. He named it Legosville, but when we saw the maps he drew, we realized that it was very similar to San Diego. That was when he told us about Mexilego, another city just below Legosville. We could see the connection between where he lived in San Diego and the Mexican border to the south.

He also continued drawing pictures of Legosville, including maps of the roads and highways. Everything had a name and a story in his town. He found a website that allowed him to generate and print road signs. Once he found this new outlet, he included an imaginary interstate that ran through the town. He also drew maps for the other imaginary cities around Legosville.

Soon after this, Tam noticed how J.T. drew, took pictures and told stories about his little town. She had set up a personal website for herself, so she decided to set up one for J.T. so he could tell people about Legosville. Then she sat with him and recorded his stories. This really excited him, so he took more pictures of this setup. He even came up with a newspaper, *The Legosville Times,* that detailed the town's news and current events. Tam would put those stories on a webpage and publish them for him.

Once he saw his website start to develop, he began adding to Legosville in earnest. He drew more maps, wrote a history of Mexilego, defined buildings, built a Legosville Transit Authority and television station, and added other bits and pieces to flesh it out. He especially enjoyed making the maps and highways. He kept himself busy by modifying the buildings, moving things around, tearing things down and eventually building new items—just like a real city.

The site is still up, even though he hasn't added anything for several years. All the graphics, pictures and drawings were created by J.T. between the ages of eleven and fifteen. He eventually lost interest in Legosville, but he continued to build models. Two of these depicted spaceships—the X-77 and the X-78—and were intricately designed down to the last detail: bridge, warp engines, sickbay, living quarters and other details befitting an interstellar vehicle. He took pictures of the entire setup and by this time he had published his own pages on the website. Tam helped by modifying his pictures and adding outer space backgrounds. He took all of the pictures and put them on the website himself. These models weren't small, either. They were about five feet long and two feet wide.

While building with his LEGO bricks, he was more interested in shape and function. Color didn't seem to interest him. He didn't use the same color for sections of his models—he simply picked out the right size and shape and used it. That was another oddity: Where other children might choose bricks of the same or similar color to coordinate the look, J.T. simply didn't care which color was used, because it just wasn't relevant to that application.

He also built one more model during this time—an oil rig. He had found out that a neighbor down the street once worked on a rig in the North Sea, so J.T. decided to build one with his LEGO bricks. In a span of two days, he built a three-foot-high model of an oil rig based solely on pictures he found on the Internet. It was complete with people, cars, piping and a little cart. There was an amazing amount of detail that exactly duplicated what he saw in the website's image. We invited the neighbor over to see the model, and he was impressed and touched that J.T. had built this for him. He said it captured a lot of the detail that was similar to the platform where he had worked. Tam took a few pictures of it, but for some reason J.T. tore down the model within a day or so. It was a little disappointing to us that he tore it down but he needed the LEGO bricks for some other project.

During this period of time, we experienced a great upsurge in J.T.'s learning and creativity. I continued reading to him while Tam worked with him on the LEGO articles. We had found yet another path for him to venture into the world–an outlet for expressing emotion through his stories about Legosville–and Tam was instrumental in helping him with the website and the stories.

Tamara

When John-John was between six and ten, he enjoyed the outdoors and he liked to be active. I only remember snippets from this time period, since John spent more time with him than I did. I was busy working a 40-hour job again and learning about the newly formed World Wide Web (WWW). A great deal of stress came with my job and I spent much of my time in the evenings relaxing in another room just to unwind. John-John would sometimes play in the same room and he liked to watch me play games on the computer. However, I tended to become a bit too involved in the games and I sometimes got upset when I was losing, so he would run away, but I don't blame him. Other times, he would sit in the room with me and play with his Brio train set or his toy cars while I spent time on the computer.

I do remember the "swamp" and how much John-John liked to play in it, which made me happy. Plus, his outdoor adventures gave me stories to tell to other parents I worked with. I enjoyed when I could feel like a normal parent and tell stories about my child's antics. Other times, I would be upset because I thought he was wasting water or that the yard looked so awful because of his excavations, but a part of me understood this was important to him and I needed to support it. When I was younger, I also liked to dig in the dirt and play in the water, so I had to remind myself to be patient with our son. I also recalled that normal kids can be hard on a house and yard, but they all eventually grow up and grow out of the behaviors that seemed like such a problem when they were younger.

As he got older, his interests did change and evolve. He played inside more, although he still needed to go outside and run around to burn off his extra energy. I remembered that my brother and I liked playing with LEGO bricks when we were growing up, so as he became older, we picked up some LEGO sets for him. However, he wasn't very interested at first and he let me put together the first few sets we got him for Christmas or his birthday. Eventually he became interested and asked for sets or buckets of them. He started to put together his own creations, but he only did this in between his other activities. As he grew older, he became even more interested and we continued to add to his LEGO collection. I thought he would use his imagination if he had something besides the kits to build with. As time passed, he built more and became very enthusiastic about his projects.

During John-John's building years, The LEGO Group opened a theme park near San Diego. It was the very first one that the company had established outside of Europe. John-John was the perfect age for the park, so I bought a yearly membership for him and myself. John would go with us every now and then, but he preferred to enjoy some time to himself while I took our son on outings. He also wasn't as interested in LEGO bricks or the park, but I enjoyed the new models and Miniland–an area with replicas of well-known locations from the real world–when we visited. Every Saturday for more than a year, John-John and I would drive from San Diego to Carlsbad so he could walk around LEGOLAND and see the sights. Of course, the big finale each week would involve me buying more LEGO sets so he could add to his city.

John-John and I did not have a chance to spend much time together, since I was usually busy with work, so we made the most of our LEGOLAND experiences. Sometimes John-John would get on the rides, but most of the time he just wanted to have lunch at Pizza Mania, walk around and spend time looking at the scale models in

Miniland. He usually got LEGO kits, but every so often he liked the LEGO bricks-by-the-pound at one of the shops. For the most part, he remained calm during these visits and there wasn't too much unusual behavior. Occasionally he would hum or run ahead of me, but most of the time we didn't draw too much attention as we walked about.

He and I enjoyed these trips very much, but they were quite expensive with the purchase of lunch and at least one LEGO set each week. In 2002, I was laid off from my job, so the outings stopped. I found new work eventually, but I had to take a pay cut, so we could not go back except for special occasions like his birthday. We dropped the yearly membership and went back to the park once or twice a year over the next few years. It seemed to work out, though, because his interests had become more diverse by then and our time together changed as well. It was another indication that he was growing up.

The LEGO years remind me of the Christmas when John-John was almost twelve and the miniature city he built in our living room. For some reason, he had suddenly decided to fill a table with model buildings. I was a bit annoyed with the setup at first, but I figured he would get bored with it all and move on to something else. Then my husband went out and bought him a couple of tables to put together, and John-John proceeded to create roads and buildings to complete his town.

Since it was Christmas, the town had to have snow, so the cotton from our manger scene under the tree was requisitioned and repositioned in the city of Legosville. We had vacationed sometime within the past year and stayed at several Motel 6s along the way, so his town boasted a Motel 9 and a restaurant. His project began to impress me, especially when he explained the detail. John-John even had a tiny photo of his dad in front of the Motel 9 and billed John as the "founder" of the chain—and for every little person and object on that table, there was a story.

Then his interest changed: right after Christmas, John-John became bored with his city and he staged a huge "fire" that swept through Legosville. He had taken an interest in my new digital camera, so he snapped pictures of the town before and after the pseudo-blaze. The cotton and glitter "snow" became smoke from the fire that swept through the city. Several buildings were toppled over and, for some reason, LEGO bricks had to be strewn about the table due to the catastrophic destruction. I thought he would tear down all of the buildings and move onto another project, as he had done with so many others before this one. However, he once again became keenly absorbed with the town, even deciding to rebuild it and make up more stories about the reconstruction. He told them as if they had been written by reporters working for *The Legosville Times*, which I think was loosely based on the daily paper our family subscribed to. I don't remember where I got the idea, but I decided to work with John-John on publishing the stories on a website. At the time, I was quite interested in web development and had my own page on the web. The host allowed several sites on the same account, so I was able to set up John-John's website and only had to pay for the domain registration.

This was before the days of Word Press, Joomla, Drupal and other content management software for website postings. At the time, the only software options were very primitive or weren't developed at all, so I created HTML pages by hand for his website. This involved opening up a text editor, tagging the content for his stories, adding links for his pictures and testing the HTML pages in a browser on my computer. Once I was satisfied that the page would display correctly, I updated the home page with a link to the webpage. I would upload the page to the website, and test again to make sure everything had uploaded and could be viewed in a web browser. We would sit together in the evenings and I listened as he told stories about Legosville. He also gave me pictures and I used a paint program to make them look like images of a LEGO city instead of the model in our back room. After I modified his pictures, I would listen and write down his stories. Next, I would add HTML tags to the text and post them on his website. As I captured his stories in HTML, I would ask him questions to clarify or add detail to the event. Legosville had moved into our patio area by then, so now he had more room to build on the project. And Legosville did expand—it spread out and gradually grew from one table to six. His little city existed for several years, and he spent a lot of time adding and removing buildings and roads. John-John was always tweaking it, tearing down buildings and putting up new ones. That first year saw the introduction of his newspaper and the happenings in the town. The project kept him busy as he explored new ways to build LEGO bricks and tell stories about them to John and myself.

In February, shortly after John-John turned twelve, we saw a news story about a young girl from San Diego who disappeared. She had been in her home at night and in the morning her parents couldn't find her. Local authorities conducted one of the biggest searches in state history. Eventually, a neighbor was suspected of abducting her while they slept. Even before any suspect was announced, much concern was raised over the possibility of someone abducting children from their homes. John-John still didn't communicate very well at the time, but I could tell from reading his Legosville stories that he was concerned over what was happening. Around the time of the abduction, John-John started telling me stories for *The Legosville Times* about a man who showed up in Legosville and went on a rampage, running over people and hurting them. While the real local newspaper and TV stations ran stories about the missing girl, John-John continued telling his stories about a crime wave in his imaginary town.

Near the end of February, the little girl's story ended on a sad note: Her body was found in a remote location of San Diego. Coincidentally, on the day the body was found, the neighbor originally suspected of the crime was arrested for her abduction and murder. John-John and I watched the news and I remember the shots from the helicopter showing the area where her body was found. Shortly after this, John-John told me a story about a memorial service in Legosville for one of the young victims and showed me pictures of the Legosville people standing for the service.

On a more personal note, the same day the body was found, I was told that I had been laid off from my company. This wrapped up a very depressing February, but we were all glad to finally see an end to the month and the bad news that year. My lack of employment proved to be a financial hardship for our family, but it benefited my son, since I now had more time to help him with his website. During the next few months, while I was out of work, he came up with more stories and I posted them along with his pictures. I continued writing his stories and asking questions to help add detail.

The events of 9/11 the year before was a traumatic event for John-John. It made quite an impression on him and he even used the tragedy to create another bad guy in Legosville whom he called Jaca Sim Baden. This shadowy figure was reportedly responsible for the Christmas fire in John-John's small town. Other villains appeared and more innocent Legosville citizens were affected by all these evildoers. He had names for all of his villains and reposted on them as they caused riots, stole things, burned the town and kidnapped people. The mayhem continued until August, when he built the Bailey Towers, two enormous structures that symbolized the rebuilding of Legosville and also served as a memorial to the World Trade Center. As I captured each story, I watched as he worked through his feelings about the upheavals in his life. This included my layoff, 9/11, the girl's kidnapping, the death of the family dog who had lived with us for John-John's entire life, and other major events that occurred during 2001 and 2002. The bad guys were eventually caught, and the kidnapped little boy was rescued.

As the year wound down, John-John told a story about the elections. He took a picture of the Bailey Towers for election night and asked me to add a full moon to it. It seemed to symbolize that a sense of peace had returned to Legosville—and to him. Then the tales began to taper off as he moved on to other interests. He kept up his additions to Legosville and its modification continued over the next several years. The stories dwindled each year until he finally moved on to his next website. These stories can be viewed at http://www.bricksville.net/. I still host the site for him, even though his time is now otherwise occupied.

Our son was growing up fast and demonstrating in his own way that he wanted independence from mom and dad. As the LEGO years drew to a close, John-John entered his teen phase and experimented in expressing his own opinions instead of echoing ours. I enjoyed this phase of his life. Sometimes there were annoyances and it was still frustrating to communicate with him; however, he continued to find new and different ways to connect with us so we could understand how he felt. These experiences helped provide a foundation. As he became a teenager, we all had to deal with some rough times in the next phase of his life.

Figure 30 – Model of an Oil Drilling Platform J.T. Built as a Project for a Neighbor

Figure 31 – Legosville with Paintshop Pro Used to Create a Night Scene

John M. Harpster & Tamara Harpster

Resources, References, and Reflections –
Special Interests

Many children on the autism spectrum have multiple special interests. To many normal people, these interests can seem obsessive and/or abnormal. However, if the child is prevented from pursuing these special interests, it can lead to a great deal of conflict. In my opinion, the child pursues a special interest because it is an area they understand and where they can exercise some measure of control. For a child on the spectrum, the world can be a confusing and frightening place. By having a special interest on which to focus, it can reduce their fears and anxieties. If parents and caregivers are willing to give support for the special interest, they may find a path to communicate with the child. I don't feel that this means the child can always have their own way, just that parents and caregivers should be willing to compromise and recognize when a child is trying to cope with the confusing world around them. The following references and resources provide examples of autistic children and how their special interests have helped them reach out to the world.

22 Words. "This Dad Knew Exactly What To Do When His Autistic Son No Longer Qualified For Services". N.p., 2015. Web. 3 Nov. 2015.

Autism.ehoow.net. "How To Explain Autism To People ." N.p., 2015. Web. 3 Nov. 2015.

Mom. "To The Stranger Who Gave Me 'The Look' When My Son Had A Public Meltdown." *The Mighty*. N.p., 2014. Web. 3 Nov. 2015.

Monsebraaten, Laurie."Autistic Man's Gift For IKEA Assembly Turns Into Business". Toronto Star, *thestar.com*. N.p., 2015. Web. 3 Nov. 2015.

News, ABC. "Health Index." *ABC News*. N.p., 2015. Web. 3 Nov. 2015.

Padawer, Ruth. "The Kids Who Beat Autism." *Nytimes.com*. N.p., 2014. Web. 3 Nov. 2015.

Seriously Not Boring. "The Story Behind 'Sea Lion Shadow.'" N.p., 2014. Web. 3 Nov. 2015.

Solomon, Andrew. "Love, No Matter What." *New.ted.com*. N.p., 2015. Web. 3 Nov. 2015.

The Huffington Post. "Dear 'Daddy' In Seat 16C." N.p., 2015. Web. 3 Nov. 2015.

Ultratesting.us. "ULTRA Testing" N.p., 2015. Web. 3 Nov. 2015.

10

The Start of the Teen Years

John

Early in 2003, J.T. turned thirteen. It was as if a switch had been flipped and the teen mode had been turned on. He stayed in his room by himself, didn't listen to his mother or me, and began to show his desire for independence. He also took to calling his mother "Tam," which upset her. I was always "Dad" to him, but J.T. seemed more inclined to use her name. He may also have been copying me. When talking to him, I referred to her as Tam and while she called me Dad, he felt that "Tam" was the correct name to use and not "Mom," so that was what he used even if she objected.

He also talked a lot more than before, but he had problems with the correct usage of pronouns, especially "I" and "you." He constantly referred to himself as "you"—as in "you'd like to go for a ride"—when he really meant "I'd like to go for a ride." Another odd speech pattern he acquired was to say he did not want to perform an activity, when in fact he really did want to. For example, he would say, "You don't want to go for a ride now," when what he really meant was "I am ready to go out right now and drive around. Please take me somewhere."

A part of his independent nature made itself known when he wanted us to leave him alone at home. I love my son, but sometimes I do need a break from it all. I'd be relieved of my duties in the evening when Tam came home, but I also started letting him stay at home by himself for short periods. I ran errands without having to worry about J.T. melting down and interfering with the grocery shopping. He wanted to learn how to ride a bicycle, so we bought him one and he learned in just one weekend. He rode all around our neighborhood, which allowed me yet another breather.

However, these two acts caused a temporary rift between Tam and me. I was fine with leaving J.T. at home for an hour or so, but Tam worried about him hurting himself or causing some form of destruction in the house. Tam was fine with him roaming around on his bicycle, but I expressed concern over his possibly being picked up by the police. I suppose she just didn't understand my worries. We did eventually see each other's viewpoints, but at the time it caused some friction between us.

As I knew it would, the bicycle caused the most problems, but it also had its benefits. On one of his first rides, he went over the handlebars and scraped both knees and his knuckles. He has always preferred to wear shorts, which meant that his knees and legs didn't have any protection from the sidewalk. Luckily he had worn a helmet, so he didn't hurt his head, but he was a sight when he came home. I was proud that he made his own way back, because the tumble occurred a couple of miles away. When he walked in, he had blood smeared everywhere: on both hands, his knees and his shins. On his way home, he had stopped at a convenience store and bought the only bandages they had in stock, little tiny ones that would do well for a small paper cut. He used several of the bandages on his hands and a few of them on one knee. For the other knee, he had taken off a sock and wrapped it around his leg in order to stop the bleeding. He had tried to clean up a bit, but he was still a real mess. Tam gasped when she saw him and asked what had happened but then calmed down when she knew he was all right. After we cleaned him up and liberally applied antibiotics and larger bandages, he looked a lot better. After all of that, he still wanted to ride his bike. He must have learned something from the incident, because that was the only time he ever came in so beaten up from bike riding.

Over the next year, he continued riding and gaining more confidence. Both of us had been allowed to roam when we were children, so neither of us was too worried after that first incident. At one point, he had ridden for several miles and was out of contact with us, since this was before the era of small cell phones. At first he carried a long-range walkie–talkie, but those became less useful as his rides took him farther away. Tam and I became more comfortable with it all, even as he started riding farther away from home. However, a couple of incidents still scared us.

A few months after he first started riding his bike, I heard him telling Tam that he needed a new rear wheel. She asked him why, since it was still fairly new. He said, "The tire is bent because a car hit me." Dogs and extraterrestrials could have heard Tam shriek at his response. It turned out that he had been clipped as he crossed an intersection at the shopping center up the street. Since he had come home on his own and wasn't in need of hospital care, I figured he hadn't been hit too hard, but Tam told him that he needed to be more careful when there were cars around.

He eventually learned to watch out for traffic, but it took another lesson before that really sank in. He tried to downplay it but wasn't very successful. When he came in this time, he once again said that he needed a new tire. One more time, his mother asked him why and he quietly answered that it was bent. This led to another round of questioning. He mumbled something about being hit by another car, but I can't be sure. It was hard to hear anything over Tam yelling, "You did *what*?!"

Fortunately for our son and our bank account, he stopped wrecking his bicycle, but he continued to ride every day. He even got to know some of the boys in the neighborhood and interacted with them. While his speech was still rudimentary, we started to notice improvements and that he seemed a bit more confident.

However, that didn't last long. Another mishap changed the way he viewed one of his favorite activities. He came home very upset about a boy who had deliberately run into him and bent another of his bike's rims. I took him to the house where the boy lived, but the mother said her son wouldn't do anything like that. I was very much the angry father, so I probably scared her and her son, but I was also upset about my boy being hurt. Since J.T. still experienced problems communicating, we never got the full story, but he didn't show the same interest in bike riding for several years.

We think there may also have been some taunting and bullying involved that made him reluctant to go back and possibly be picked on again. After that day, J.T. no longer wanted to go out and ride his bike. A couple of weeks later, some of the other boys came by the house to ask him to ride with them, but he refused even when Tam and I tried to talk him into it. For the next few years he was reluctant to leave the house, even just to walk around the block. He also did not look for other kids to play or ride with. There was a boy about his age who lived a couple of houses down from us, but J.T. showed no interest in trying to make friends with him. He did start riding his bike again a few years later, but not with other kids in the neighborhood.

We lived far from any family and neither of us was very good at making friends, so we took care of J.T. by ourselves. For many years, we stayed at home, not trusting babysitters due to the challenges that his meltdowns and behavior presented. Since neither Tam nor I are very interested in going out a lot, we didn't notice too much of a loss, but we did miss going out on dates as we did before we had J.T. Once we felt comfortable with leaving him at home alone, we established a weekly date night. We really enjoyed the down time with each other after so many years of focusing on our son's needs. Our dates were simple: We went to a local restaurant and we were only gone for about an hour–two at the most–but it was a major milestone for us.

We didn't stay away from the house very long each week and were confident that J.T. would be okay when we returned, although one night we wondered what we would find at the house when, on the way home, we saw police helicopters circling around our neighborhood. It turned out that a prisoner had escaped from a downtown courtroom and was seen in our vicinity. We were glad that the incident did not involve J.T., but we certainly wondered what we would find as we got closer to our house and the aircraft circled the area.

When J.T. was around fourteen or fifteen, he became more difficult to handle. He was going through the physical changes of adolescence, but he still didn't possess the understanding or communication skills to deal with what was happening to him. We found ourselves emotionally handicapped when trying to talk to him about his changes and did the best we could to support him during his rough time. Being a teenager is tough enough for normal kids who have more experience in communicating and expressing their feelings.

Take away communication and social skills and the teen years can be, in a word, interesting.

J.T. was still trying to figure himself out and what he liked didn't always coincide with what we thought might be best for him. He and his mother are very much alike, and this has led to some spectacular "discussions" (i.e. yelling and door-slamming) between them. I was usually able to remain neutral, but sometimes J.T. could test even my patience and push me over the edge.

Some issues during this time revolved around us showing J.T. how to redirect his anger and not take it out on objects or people. He hadn't reached his full physical growth yet, but it wasn't any fun when we were hit as he swung his arms during a tantrum. Tam and I worked with him and tried to teach him to walk away from situations that made him angry–and especially to not strike other people. We also taught him not to throw things or tear them apart, but our main priority at that time involved showing him that hurting people was never acceptable.

When he was fourteen, he decided to start a new website called JJ98. He took an online nickname based on what we called him, John-John, and the number 98. The nickname caught on in the late nineties when Windows 98 had first been released. He was interested in the new operating system as well as the number, so he decided to combine them. When he started his website, he named it *jj98.com*, and then changed it to *johnjohn98.com*. Tam again set it up for him, but this time she used software that would allow him to upload text and pictures to the site by himself. Then she turned over most of the control to him.

Tamara

On John-John's thirteenth birthday, my mother had come to visit, as usual, and we all had a good time. He smiled for the camera and looked quite happy, but he also began staying in his room more often with the door closed. He had liked spending time with me in the evenings before that, but when he became a teen, this changed. It's hard to explain, but I felt that he wanted to be away from me. As a mom, I understand that this is a natural part of growing up, but that didn't make it any easier to accept at the time.

During his fourteenth year, his interests also shifted from Legosville to building spaceship models. He still took many pictures, but now they consisted of the X-77 and X-78 craft he built with his LEGO bricks. Both spaceships were large, about four feet long, two feet wide and very detailed. His articles about Legosville became less frequent, while stories about the spaceships increased. It seemed like his fascination with LEGO bricks had slowed as he explored other areas.

Toward the end of 2003, a large wildfire in San Diego, called the Cedar Fire, threatened many families' homes countywide, including ours. For several days, everyone in the area closely monitored the blaze as it inched closer to the city. John-John was strongly affected by this and spent a lot of time processing the event. However, there was no need to write Legosville articles about this event as he had about the kidnapping and murder of that poor little girl two years before. In many ways, he was growing up, although his communication skills still did not match those of his peers.

I don't remember much about his fourteenth year, except that he kept trying new things and expanding his interests. During that time, he decided that he wanted to set up a separate website from his LEGO bricks site. For this new venture, he used his online nickname, JohnJohn98. Here he wrote about cartoons, science fiction and other interests. I set up another website and registered a domain name for him. I also used software for the site that allowed him to update it without my help. It was a bit scary to give him the freedom to update the website on his own, but he wanted to do it and he did fine. I was worried about him posting on the website, breaking it or melting down when he couldn't fix it. After some spectacular meltdowns when the Internet had gone down, I did not look forward to his behavior if his website did not work whenever he chose to look it over. Fortunately, the software I chose was stable and he was not upset because his website had broken. However, if the Internet went down and he couldn't get to the site, it could get unpleasant as John or I worked to distract him.

Sometime after he began the new website, John-John came up with an idea for a movie titled *The Robot Man*. He based it on a combination of the *Terminator* and *Robocop* franchises. He drew posters and designed CD covers for the movie. He created storyboards on the sheets of paper as he laid out the story. He also took an interest in stop-motion filming and used his LEGO mini-figures as the actors. He filmed a few scenes, carefully setting up each scene with sets built from LEGO bricks. I found it interesting that he started using the same color when making his little buildings and rooms. Somehow he noticed that this setup would look better if they were the same color, so he started to build them that way. Just like his characters in *The Legosville Times*, all the characters in this story had a name, background and history. However, this project is one that he worked on all by himself. I would hear bits and pieces, but I didn't hear all of his stories as I had when he worked on the newspaper.

He also rode his bicycle a lot during this phase of his life and, as a result, got to know some of the neighborhood boys. I was really glad to see him getting out of the house and meeting people. I even noticed a difference in how he talked after this had begun. Now it was more of a conversation instead of a monologue, since there were other people where he could gain new ideas. His pronoun usage also improved, as well as other subtle speech patterns. I will admit that I wasn't too happy when he came in and said he had been hit by a car. I later realized that he had only been clipped by a car bumper while crossing the street on his bike, not that a car had actually run into him head-on. However, his language, "a car hit me," certainly got my attention—both times it happened. Otherwise, I was just happy that he was learning more about the outside world.

Unfortunately, one or two of the boys he had befriended decided to pick on him. I was at work when I got a call from John about the incident. John-John had come home very upset, especially since his bike rim had been bent yet again. He told us that they ran into him on purpose and warped the rear wheel on his bike. In the evening, after I came home, John told me about how he had attempted to resolve the situation but didn't have any luck. He had gone over to the house that John-John pointed out and tried to talk to the mother. John-John was with him and had pointed out the house where the boy was supposed to live. The mother answered the door and John explained what had happened, and asked to see her son to ask him about the incident. The mother stayed at the door and told John that her son didn't do anything. John repeated the story and asked how they were going to pay for the bicycle repair, but the mother was adamant that her son had not done anything to John-John. Eventually, John walked away unsatisfied with the solution, but there was not anything else we could do. We did get the rim repaired so John-John could ride his bicycle again.

I did try to talk with John-John about the incident, but I couldn't get any more information. He would simply run off–his standard method of avoiding a discussion. Because of our difficulties communicating with him, John and I could not be sure about what had happened and we did not see any point in trying to pursue the matter. We both could see that it would end up poorly, since John-John could not communicate well and he might not be believed.

After this happened he didn't ride his bike again for a long time. He had enjoyed it so much that I tried to encourage him, but I did not push because I knew it would upset him. A couple of weeks later, when he had not gone outside at all, some of the boys stopped by to ask him to come riding. I was able to get him to the door and I hoped that seeing that the boys were interested in him might convince him to get back out there with them. However, he simply greeted the boys, told them he didn't want to play anymore and went to his room. I was proud that he stayed calm, but also disappointed that he did not want to go out to play. I thanked the boys for stopping by and they left. They seemed disappointed that John-John wouldn't go with them. At the time, I thought perhaps they were disappointed because they might have missed his company. I certainly hope it wasn't because they wouldn't have him around to pick on or take advantage of him.

I wish that he had gone with the boys, but after my childhood of suffering from bullying and teasing, I understood why he would not want to take another chance to be picked on or bullied. I also knew that there may have been other problems and this incident was simply the final straw for my son. Just as I did not have the skills or confidence to step up to bullying, my son did not have any skills either and I did not have the experience to advise him on how to handle these types of situations.

It hurt me to see him like this, but I didn't know what to do to get him to trust other kids his age. Forcing him would have resulted in meltdowns and since he was so much bigger, John and I could no longer push him into activities as we had when he was younger. Because of my issues with socialization, I didn't have any good advice to give him, so he went back to staying in the house and occasionally riding his bike, but no longer venturing out to meet people.

He still liked to play in the back yard and run around at night, especially in the summer evenings when it was cooler. However, he also hummed louder during this time, so I worried that he might annoy the neighbors if he was outside after ten. Because of this, I set a curfew for him. He had to be in the house by ten at night so he wouldn't bother the neighbors. By this time, he understood us much better, so it only took one or two nights of reminding him to come in. One night, while he splashed around in his wading pool, something seemed off, so I went out to check on him. Imagine my surprise when I found him in his pool–stark naked!

He had somehow decided that clothes or a swimsuit weren't needed for swimming, so he sat in his pool without a stitch of clothing. If he had stayed in the pool, that might not have been so bad, but every now and then he would get up to run around, so I hauled him into the house and told him that he had to wear his swim trunks because other people might see him, even at night. Our house was backed by an alley and because of his size, I didn't want someone calling the police and reporting him for indecent exposure. Because of my reaction, it only took once to learn that lesson, but I did keep an eye on him from then on, just in case he decided he would prefer to run around *sans* clothes again.

In other areas, he showed more interest in responsibility. For many years, we had a large projection TV, but we had not watched it very much. The set was an early model and the picture was faded. I did not watch much TV, so it just sat in our living room unused for many years. We decided to sell it and eventually got rid of it sometime in 2004. However, apparently John-John felt that a proper house needed a TV, along with a sound system. John and I gave him an allowance and he started saving it up. Over the space of several months, he saved enough money to buy a new TV, stereo, VHS player, cassette player, CD player and a mixer for a media center. He bought this for the family, even though John and I told him that he didn't have to do this. As he pieced together the system, he set it up in the living room, connected the wires and even included a small surround-sound system for our living room. For the money, it was a nice setup and we did occasionally watch movies together. However, what I was most impressed with was his saving the money, picking the components and assembling them into a complete system.

He also chose to work on another project for his room around this time. He had a TV in his room and many items scattered about. The house was very small, so there wasn't a lot of storage space. On his own, he designed a set of shelves with cabinets that would hold his TV, cassette tapes, CDs and other media. He drew a picture of it and measurements for the shelves, and then he and John bought wood at the hardware store and built the shelves. He sanded everything and stained it, and when the project was completed it didn't look too bad. When they finished, it fit perfectly in his room in the spot he had chosen for it. We still have the shelves, although they are a little beat up after ten years, and they provide a nice storage place for our spare bedroom.

John-John began to focus more on his JohnJohn98 website and less on the Legosville website. Around this time, he discovered Wikipedia and submitted articles. I don't know much about the content of what he submitted or what the discussions were like for him online. As someone who is comfortable with computers, I could have set up monitoring software, but I decided to model how I was raised and respect his privacy, unless given cause to look for problems. I would occasionally check online to see what was happening with his profile, but otherwise I stayed out of it. I knew he would need to learn how to deal with people and that he could gain valuable experience by writing these articles.

I know from my later searches that many of his articles were rejected. At the time, he would become frustrated and run around the house, occasionally banging on things to get over his anger. I believe that some of his articles were accepted, but Wikipedia is notorious for its choosiness and less-than-tactful handling of new submissions. Based on later blog entries of his, I know that this made him feel bad, but I also realize that this was one way for him to find out about the real world—and that not all people would treat him nicely. Part of my job as a parent has involved learning when to step in and protect my son, and when to step back and let him experience the world. He had to learn that not everyone will act well. It can be a hard line to walk and I'm still learning.

We also experienced an incident where John-John was contacted by someone about a gaming article he had posted on his site. He had apparently copied it from Wikipedia and the owner contacted us about the information. I feared the worst, but it turned out that the creator of the game just wanted to make sure the information was updated to reflect his latest press releases. I wrote back and promised that we would update the site and reference theirs as well. As a thank-you, he sent John-John some preview pictures of the game that he could use on his site.

I was very much relieved, since I know that copyright infringement is taken very seriously on the Internet. I have also drilled this information into my son so that he may be more aware of different copyright licenses and that he is not supposed to copy anything unless it is allowed by a Creative Commons license for the item, similar to what Wikipedia uses. In some ways, he could be very responsible, once he was aware of an issue. However, he still hummed, stomped his feet and shook his head when angry about things he couldn't control. While his speech had improved and he could express himself in complete sentences, we still didn't always understand what he was talking about. Just like many other teenagers, he was a mix of childish behavior and maturity, with autism adding an interesting flavor to his behavior.

Figure 32 – Model of the X-78 Spaceship Merged with an Outer
Space Background

Figure 33 – Reverse Angle of the X-78

John M. Harpster & Tamara Harpster

Figure 34 – Logo for the *X-78* Movie

Figure 35 - Galley Inside the X-78

Resources, References, and Reflections – The Teen Years

During the teen years, parenting an autistic child can have additional challenges. Even though the teenager may be behind in mental and social development, the body is still developing, which can be confusing. During adolescence, children transition to adulthood physically and mentally. Clear communication and support from parents are important, but it can be difficult to achieve full communication with autistic people, depending on where they have issues. There may also be delays in behavior for autistic teens, which means they may not have developed as many skills to deal with the changes as their peers have achieved. As these peers transition and find their own place in an adult world, normal teenagers may pick on autistic teens in order to show that they are part of the normal group and not an outsider.

In addition, there may be extra stress on autistic teens due to increased expectations for mature behavior. Activities that may have seemed cute or acceptable when they were younger are now frowned upon or actively discouraged. Autistic teens may choose to change their behaviors on their own in an effort to fit in more closely with normal teenagers. However, due to the energy it takes for someone on the spectrum to act normal, autistic teens may act out more at home and experience more frequent meltdowns as they try to cope with these increased requirements for adult behavior.

I can see now that I held higher expectations for John-John's behavior as he grew older, even though I knew intellectually that he was behind in his social skills. I fell into the same trap that I was afraid other people would struggle with when meeting my son—that because he is 6'2" and physically close to adulthood, that he is also socially and mentally ready for this change. In reality, his adult body was something new that he had to learn to deal with while he was still thinking and reacting more like a ten to twelve year old. As more was expected of him, he would try to comply, but since it wasn't natural, it took more out of him and so he needed to act out more. This seemed like rebellion and defiance, but I now realize it was his coping mechanism for stress from all of the changes.

Based on what I have learned, I believe I would have lowered some of my expectations and worked to show more support for John-John as he grew and changed. For me, this would have involved a better understanding that he was feeling stressed and that I needed to be more nurturing instead of yelling or arguing about how he needed to change and act normally. I should also have worked to be more accepting of his "stims," understanding that these behaviors helped him to bleed off his stress and anxiety, which allowed him to cope with the changes brought about by adolescence. In short, I should have worked to reduce his stress so he would have more energy to listen and learn about behaviors that were truly important, instead of worrying about trivial acts that I can't even fully recall some 10 years later.

Adolescence is a time when young women who are on the spectrum may finally be diagnosed. For young girls who are verbal, they can often imitate the behavior of their peers and blend in, but when adolescence begins, they find it more difficult to imitate these behaviors. Due to these differences, they may be shunned by their peers and have difficulty connecting with others. As of 2016, it is slowly being recognized that there are more young women on the spectrum, but finding and helping them is a slow and daunting task. If they are not diagnosed, the bullying and shunning can lead to depression, anxiety and other mental health issues that will cause problems for them as adults. All autistic teens need a safe place where they can be themselves and take a break from the transition period between childhood and adulthood.

The following set of resources provides some information about the experience of adolescence for autistic teens. The focus is on positive articles to help parents and their children.

Dewey, Margaret A. and Margaret P. Everard. "The Near-Normal Autistic Adolescent" J Autism Dev Disord 4.4 (1974): 348-356. Web.

Everard, Margaret P.. "An Approach to Teaching Autistic Children": Pergamon International Library of Science, Technology, Engineering and Social Studies. Pergamon, May 2014

John M. Harpster & Tamara Harpster

ISBN: 9780080208954 (Format: PDF)
http://hcallen.jczckj.com/document/an-approach-to-teaching-autistic-children-by-margaret-p-everard.pdf (E-books Unlimited)

Grandin, Ph.D., Temple and Dera Moore, Ph.D. "The Loving Push." Arlington, Tx: Future Horizons INC, 2015. Print.

McGill University Health Centre. "Adolescence and Autism: A Difficult, But Not Hopeless Combination." ScienceDaily. ScienceDaily, 3 November 2007. <www.sciencedaily.com/releases/2007/11/071102091148.htm>.

Sarris, Marina. "Autism in the Teen Years: What to Expect, How to Help | Interactive Autism Network." Iancommunity.org. N.p., 2013. Web. 26 Apr. 2016.

Savko, Tanya. "Teen Autism: Life in the Different Lane." Teenautism.com. N.p., 2016. Web. 26 Apr. 2016.

Sicile-Kira, Chantal. "Thirteen Things Parents of Teens with Autism Need to Know: Adolescence and Autism Together Form a Volatile Mix." The Autism Advocate. N.p., 2011. Web. 26 Apr. 2016.

Wendler, Daniel. "Online Social Skills Guide – Improve Your Social Skills." Improve Your Social Skills. N.p., 2016. Web. 26 Apr. 2016.

Wolf, Anthony E. "Get Out of My Life, but First Could You Drive Me & Cheryl to the Mall: A Parent's Guide to the New Teenager." Farrar, Straus and Giroux. August 1, 2002. Print.

11

The Road to Adulthood

John

Although J.T. was a teenager physically, his interests could still be considered childish. For example, he was very interested in cartoons and watched many different shows on Cartoon Network. On his website, http://www.johnjohn98.com, he wrote articles about the shows while describing the episodes and characters. He eventually built an extensive database of articles about cartoon shows, movies and other programs. He wrote most of the text, but depended on Wikipedia for some of the articles.

While he expanded his website, I continued to read to him and look at various articles online. We continued to homeschool him even after he turned 16 and was no longer required by law to attend school. We continued to keep school hours, with J.T. remaining inside the house until 3 p.m., when most public schools finished for the day. However, as a break, I also began driving J.T. around San Diego so he could take in the sights and see all the roads he had read about in his map books and online. He continued adding to his knowledge by learning all he could about San Diego and its different attractions. He liked when we traveled the secondary highways and explored the various nooks and crannies of San Diego County. We put many miles on the family van, and J.T. enjoyed seeing all the places that he had found on his maps.

When he was fifteen, J.T. and I worked on a home project after a flooding incident in the master bathroom. Our toilet had backed up over the weekend, but we did not want to pay for a plumber to come out on a Saturday. The toilet also wouldn't shut off after a flush, which meant the water kept running. Since the plumbing was now backed up, we had to make sure it stopped running so the bathroom wouldn't flood. The toilet worked just fine for most of the weekend and we kept it from overflowing into the bathroom.

On Sunday night, Tam had awakened and got up to use the bathroom. However, she forgot to make sure the toilet stopped running before going back to bed. Since she needed background noise to help her sleep, her fan was on and she couldn't hear that the toilet was still running. About an hour after she went back to bed, J.T. woke us to say that there was water on the floor. Being awakened at 2 a.m. is no fun, but to get up to a flooded house is even worse. We shut off the water and the whole family pitched in to dry the floor before morning. Due to our previous experiences with J.T. and wet carpets, we had a shop vacuum that would suck up water anywhere in the house. I suspect that this was not a normal bonding experience for most families, but somehow it seemed normal to us at the time. After we sopped up most of the water, the room still retained that earthy aroma, so we moved into the living room and the spare bedroom for the rest of the night. J.T.'s room also had some water in it, but since the smell wasn't as bad, he was able to sleep there that evening.

Tam took the next day off so we could work together to start cleaning up the mess. We called our insurance company and a water damage cleanup service. About the time we got the quote from the cleaners, we also heard from the insurance carrier. They said they'd send someone out, but if the adjuster thought the flood was our fault, they wouldn't pay anything. Since we already knew about the bad toilet, we figured the insurance company would use this as an excuse to not pay, and we would have to cover the cleaning and repairs ourselves. The carpet cleaners had just handed us a $3,000 estimate just to strip out the carpets and remove wet drywall, and that didn't cover fixing any of the damage, so we quickly rejected their proposal and showed them the door. Tam and I decided we could do the project ourselves. We had always done our own home repairs and I had worked on construction crews before, so we knew we could get it done. We proceeded to strip out the carpeting and cut out the damaged drywall.

Over the next few months, I put up new drywall and gave the work site a fresh coat of paint. We did pay someone to install carpet in the bedrooms, but that was the only work we paid to have done for our fix-it project. With J.T's help, I finally finished everything, but the project took a lot of time. I continued to homeschool John-John during this time, but that was also slowed due to the repairs. He worked on his website and built things with his LEGO bricks, but not as much as he had done a few years earlier. And while he did not associate with other boys his age, he did start riding his bike again. He wanted to ride so much that he sometimes had problems with the rule about staying in the house until 3 p.m. After he started riding, he would become restless about an hour or so before class was supposed to end. When the clock hit 3, he would usually shoot out the door to ride. After his long break from bike riding, he now seemed determined to ride as far as he could in order to see as much of our neighborhood as he could before nightfall. There were no more incidents with cars or scrapes, so at least he had improved on that aspect of his previous riding adventures.

Our time at home must have been somewhat uneventful, because I find it harder to pull up specific memories of J.T. at this age. I have looked at numerous pictures from those years to try to spark my memory. The Christmas pictures from 2005–when J.T. was fifteen–are very interesting. One example of how he decided to show his independence–and because he had problems sitting still–was to cut his own hair. The Christmas pictures show him with the sides and top of his head shaved, while the back of his head was still covered with hair.

A few days later, he decided to even things out and just shaved his head completely. When I saw his bald head, I just asked him if he was planning to join the Marines. For once, Tam wasn't overly upset. I remember that he came up to her one evening, giggling nervously, and asked her if she thought his shaved head was stupid. She just told him that he was the one who had to live with how he looked if he shaved his head, shrugged and went back to what she was doing. J.T. didn't say anything, he just giggled. Over the next few years, he continued to shave his head periodically–usually around Christmas or his birthday. Maybe he wanted to make a statement in the pictures Tam took at each event, but he definitely wanted to show that he had control over his own hair.

Fortunately for Tam and me, J.T. began to calm down by the time he turned sixteen. He actually looked happy in those pictures, instead of always wearing a frown as he did the year before. I continued to help him with his schoolwork, but the focus was definitely reduced and there didn't seem to be as much of a push. I think our whole family had become burned out from dealing with this issue on our own for so many years.

During this time, Tam had to deal with the stress of work and an almost constant threat of being laid off. J.T. and I dealt with his changes as a teenager and my getting older.

As this project goes to press, J.T. is in his mid-twenties and still learns new things and improves on the old. Writing this book has been challenging and we both agreed that we should end it at J.T.'s teen years. We are still dealing with the challenges of autism as J.T. explores adulthood and what that means for him. There isn't a clear-cut ending here, though, just the continuing saga of our family finding new ways to cope with each other as we get older.

Part of parenthood is learning that children are not simply echoes of ourselves, but individuals with personalities all their own. This can be especially challenging with autistic children, because so much concern exists about how they will do in the real world, who will support them if something happens to the parents, and how the world will treat them considering their issues with social interaction. In our case, we are encouraged with the strides our son has made and extremely proud of his increasing maturity over the last few years. Now we feel that he is even closer to not needing us quite so much as he used to–and that independence is possible.

This is a story of how we dealt with the challenges that autism brings. We hope it may offer some insight into what our family has gone through and help people understand what other families face when raising autistic children.

Tamara

John-John at fourteen wasn't too much of a handful, but when he turned fifteen he was definitely working through some issues. Pictures from his fifteenth birthday showed that he had grown very close to his current height of 6'2". However, he was not a happy young man and was angry a lot more often. This was about the same time that he started calling me "Tam" instead of "Mom," which did hurt my feelings. I'm afraid I was not always very grown-up and occasionally I became upset when he addressed me by my first name. Most of the time, I worked to keep my anger suppressed, but it was difficult.

This was also the year when my husband explained the concept of what I call "John-John-speak." John-John speak occurs when he says he doesn't want something when he actually does. When John explained this behavior to me, it helped me to more effectively communicate with John-John, but it also bothered me because I felt like I hadn't spent enough time with my son and didn't know him as well as I should. Even harder to accept was the fact that John-John felt closer to his father than to me. A part of me just did not want to acknowledge my son's autism, which made it hard for me to accept my son as he was. Because I had problems with this, my conflicts with John-John arose because I wanted him to be something that he wasn't and it caused tension between the two of us.

Life wasn't always about conflict when John-John was fifteen. He also began projects around the yard to fix things up. He had finally outgrown his "swamp," so he filled in the area. It was all dirt and no grass, but after several years of living with a muddy, watery area, it seemed like an improvement. He decided that we needed a vegetable garden instead. Due to the rocks, toys and mess in his swamp area, I pointed him to another corner of the back yard and he began to remove the grass. We rented a rototiller to turn the dirt and mix in topsoil we had bought. We bought seeds for corn, beans, lettuce and other vegetables.

The snails ate the lettuce after it grew, the corn never grew very tall and the beans dried out because we kept forgetting to water them. I think we saw one tiny ear of corn that year. John-John was still interested in the garden the next year, but it was even less successful than the first year. During this time, John-John asked us to buy bricks so he could place them around the back yard as ornamentation. They turned out to be more of an annoyance, because now we had to lift the lawnmower over them. But they did make the yard look neater.

Occasionally, we would leave him at home by himself for longer times, which helped us cope with handling his issues. Being able to have a dinner night off once a week gave both of us a second wind to deal with him. Due to our concern for his care, these were the only breaks we both had together while we took care of him. Fortunately, both of us are introverts and didn't mind staying at home most of the time, but after so many years of caring for John-John, we both enjoyed–and needed–a break in our routine.

The year he turned fifteen brought other changes as well, in our home and with John. In May our bathroom flooded, so we needed to remove the carpet and take out the wet drywall, among other repairs. After we called the insurance company and found out they might not pay for the damage, John and I decided to do the work ourselves–which meant that John would do most of the work and I would cheer him on. I did help on the first day of the flood by staying home and working with John to remove the wet carpet from the house. After that, John and John-John cut out the wet drywall in the flooded rooms. At least we had learned how much drywall should be cut when we were given the cleaning estimate. John focused on getting John-John's room back in shape, since he could get very agitated if he didn't have everything as he expected.

During this time I came down with a nasty stomach flu. It was so bad that I actually missed a week of work and still felt low for another week or two after I returned to my job. I remember being so sick in that empty bedroom. The missing drywall only served to remind me that I just wished things could be fixed—not just in our house, but in our family life as well. I finally got over that virus and everything returned to normal, but by then I was ready for some kind of change. I just hoped it was sooner rather than later.

I also noticed a change in John. I started to realize that I had not helped enough at home and the years of caring for John-John had taken a toll on my husband. Since John is fourteen years older, I was concerned that something had gone wrong that could affect our family. At first I wasn't sure what to do, but eventually I picked up some of the chores that John had been performing. Laundry, meal-planning and grocery lists were now my tasks. Whenever I called him to let him know I was coming home late, I kept the meals simple so John would just have to reheat them.

I also took over the finances by paying the bills and monitoring the checkbook. I had to grow up some and help out around the house instead of depending on John to do everything in addition to taking care of John-John. It was a hard time for me, for up to that point I had focused on work. I started to realize that I had been taking advantage of the situation and that John was paying the price with his health. I knew that this must change, so over the next few years I continued to do more at home.

This paid off in the long run and I feel that our family is stronger now as a result—so much so that I'm now participating more fully in taking care of J.T. and the house. In the meantime, John continued to work with John-John and help him out with his interests as they came and went. They even drove all over San Diego on excursions planned by John-John.

In the meantime, our home life continued to change. Our beagle dog, Misty, passed away when John-John was eleven. He was fifteen when we got a cat. I liked pets, but I didn't want another dog because I knew I wouldn't have time to properly take care of it. John-John had been asking about getting another pet in the years after our dog died, but it wasn't until he was fifteen that he became more persistent about it. He had originally asked for a dog, but I talked him into getting a cat instead. We went down to the shelter to find one, but John-John wouldn't go, so John and I picked out our cat.

Or I should say that she chose us. She was lonely and super-friendly and we just knew John-John would take to her, so we brought her home and introduced her to him as Kala. Unfortunately, Kala and John-John did not get along as well as we had originally thought. The next few months were pretty interesting as he and Kala got to know each other. They did finally come to an understanding, but I wasn't sure who would survive, as John-John tried to make friends with her in the same way he had with our dog. His idea was to roughhouse with her, pet her somewhat vigorously and squeeze her tightly as he tried to hold her. Since she was a cat, she had claws and she used them, after which she would run and hide under a bed or behind boxes to get away from him. For a few months, he wore claw marks on his arms, but as the time passed, these were fewer as he figured out that he needed to use a gentler approach.

John-John had begun to act more responsibly, but we still dealt with some rough spots. One of these was increased expenses. As a youngster, he loved to treat his bed like a trampoline. Naturally, as he got older and heavier, the bed would break on a pretty regular basis. He also liked to spin around in his chair, which also eventually broke. After three years of replacing his chair every six months and his bed every year, I finally put my foot down and said, "No more!"

Of course, my foot notwithstanding, he didn't change his behavior patterns overnight. He had to put up with a broken chair and bed for a time, until the chair was so badly wrecked that he could no longer sit at his desk. We bought him a new chair, but I told him that if it didn't last at least six months, I would buy him a small pink chair that was very cheap and that's all he would have to sit on.

It took him a while, but he finally stopped spinning in his chair as much. In fact, it took him a year-and-a-half to break the new chair we had bought, so we bought him a sturdier one. He also got a new bed, but he did have to sleep on a broken frame for a time. He finally got the message when he broke a brand-new bed that John and I had bought for ourselves. We had it for only two weeks when I noticed that it sagged a lot on one side. When we looked at the box spring, we noticed the broken slats underneath and I blew up at John-John. We fixed the bed ourselves by taking off the bottom covering, pulling out the broken 1" x 2" boards and replacing them with new ones. After John-John saw us wrestling with the box spring and heard our cursing as we pulled out the broken pieces, he finally seemed to understand that he should not be as rough on the furniture. We certainly found it handy to have some repair skills for dealing with some of our son's issues.

After John-John turned sixteen, he seemed to calm down. It suddenly became a lot more pleasant around the house. I put aside my feelings of disappointment that he wasn't able to get his driver's license like other kids his age, but at least he was beginning to settle down. He started calling me Mom again, but not all of the time. We even took a trip to Texas to visit John's family and John-John didn't act too upset about the change in his routine. We packed the van with LEGO bricks, books and other items that we needed to keep him occupied, and it was a very restful trip for all of us.

We had a pleasant time for his seventeenth birthday and my mother came out for her annual visit. We have some nice family pictures from a visit to the beach and he looked like a happy young man as he hugged his Nana. Things at my work settled down some that year and it seemed to be a more positive time for our family. In October of 2007, the Witch Creek and the Harris fires burned in the San Diego area. We all watched the news and the sky as smoke filled the area in the mountains to the east and the southern part of San Diego County. However, the county was better prepared this time around and the Witch Creek fire burned in a line north of our house. John-John experienced some anxiety, but since the smoke did not flow directly over our house, he was not as anxious as he was in 2003.

By the time he reached eighteen, John-John had kept up with his classes and reading Wikipedia with his father. He also experimented with shooting stop-motion movies of his LEGO models for film ideas. But by the end of his traditional school years, we were all burned out and ready for a break from the stress of earlier times. With my job situation improving and John-John becoming calmer, it was a welcome relief for all of us, and John-John continued to mature and learn new ways to interact and deal with the world.

Resources, References, and Reflections – Transition to Adulthood

When normal children maneuver through their teen years, they prepare for an independent life at eighteen, leaving home to work, go to college, join the military or in some other way explore what it's like to take responsibility for their lives. The problems with social issues and possible lack of maturity can delay this stage for autistic people. There are currently fewer resources for young adults on the autism spectrum, which limits their choices for pursuing independent living. When looking back at John-John's teen years right before eighteen, I'm not sure what we could have done differently. Because of our approach, everyone in our family was burned out and ready for a break. Perhaps we could have worked on more life skills, the type of things that any adult needs to know in order to take care of themselves. However, I have always believed in working on life skills with children, such as cooking, cleaning, handling money and other tasks that are part of adulthood, so John-John had already been learning those traits. In my research over the past year or so, I have discovered more options for young adults with autism, but more still needs to be accomplished in this area. The focus has always been on helping autistic children with the idea that their condition can be "cured" and the child can grow and live a normal life as an adult. We have found, as many others have, that there is no cure, and no clean or simple solutions for a young adult with autism who wants independence. There is not just one solution, but many different methods of dealing with young adults who are on the spectrum and who want to move into the adult world. I have included some resources about autistic teens and adults in order to provide some examples of what these children can accomplish as they grow up.

Carlysvoice.com. "Carly's Voice | Order Yours Today!". N.p., 2015. Web. 3 Nov. 2015.

Grandin, Temple. *Temple Grandin On Working With Autism: I Like The Way I Think*. 2015. Web. 3 Nov. 2015.

Kim, Cynthia. "Musings of an Aspie". N.p. 2014. Web. https://musingsofanaspie.com.

neurowonderful. "Neurowonderful." N.p., 2015. Web. 3 Nov. 2015.

Templegrandin.com, "Welcome To Temple Grandin's Official Autism Website." N.p., 2015. Web. 3 Nov. 2015.

Afterword

John

During our life with J.T. and his autism, our family wandered many different paths to try to find ways to reach him. The first was through his drawing. He wanted to communicate with us, but did not have the language skills, so he used his pictures to reach out. Through these images, he began to communicate and gradually figured out how words could be used as a way to express himself as well. They also provided a bridge that reduced his frustration while he worked on his speech skills.

In my opinion, drawing is not the only way for autistic people to reach out to others. They can sing or use computers, for example. Humans are social creatures, so when we see children who do not seem to want to reach other people, based on our experience, we figure it is probably out of frustration or their inability to use standard methods of communicating. Maybe they have used all of their resources without success, so they withdraw. In that case, someone who cares for the child should try to reach him/her with an adult's knowledge and understanding of the situation.

Since autism runs the gamut of communication styles, personalities and reactions, it is up to the adults to make that connection happen. J.T.'s drawing was simply his way of reaching out—and it worked.

Tamara

While this is the end of our book, it is not the end of our story. As the years have passed, we have found out through experience that autism isn't cured, but it is an inherent part of the person and affects them for life. John-John continues to mature, but at a slower pace than his peers. Autism affects the entire family, and it can be terribly isolating as parents and children try to figure out the answers to their problems. As I look back at this book I've realized that its focus is on our life as a family while dealing with autism. I feel like many families become so focused on autism and the difficulties associated with it that they forget how to simply be with each other. Now that I'm older and possibly wiser, I can see that I am seeing my son as a person instead of a disorder

While we may not have wanted to travel the road of autism, somehow we have moved forward and made it to his adult years. We found some good stories along the way, took some lovely pictures and found our way together. We are still a family that cares for one other. We occasionally fight and bicker, but we make up and realize our mistakes along the way. In other words, we are a family, like so many others in the world.

After my research, and the work of putting together this book and continuing to learn about my son, I would suggest to other parents that sometimes the best thing you can do is to relax and trust that you and your child can find a way to work together. It can be too easy to focus on trying to make a child normal and it inevitably leads to creating a tense, stressful situation and an uncomfortable, unhappy home life. If I could go back and change one thing about my relationship with my son, I would relax more and not worry quite so much about what other people do or don't like about our behavior as a family. I find it encouraging that more parents are working to make people aware of the behaviors and issues of autism. Their work is helping others understand that the stress of trying to appear normal when a person has a different way of thinking causes many behaviors on the spectrum. I am optimistic that things will continue to improve and that, at some point, my son will find his own place in the world.

Resources, References, and Reflections – Adulthood and Autism

The following are some references for adults on the spectrum, including those who were diagnosed as an adult. While autistic people can appear "normal," it does not mean that they find it easy or comfortable to function in the real world. Support groups can also help with counseling for co-morbid conditions such as depression, anxiety

"You Don't Want to Go For a Ride"

and other issues that can increase the coping mechanisms an adult can use.

"Healthcare Toolki.t" Academic Autistic Spectrum Partnership in Research and Education. N.p., 2016. Web. 24 Mar. 2016.

"Your Guide To Autism Spectrum Disorders From About.Com." About.com Health. N.p., 2016. Web. 24 Mar. 2016.

Attwood, Tony. "The Complete Guide to Asperger's Syndrome." London: Jessica Kingsley Publishers, 2006. Print.

Bonnello, Chris. "Growing Up Autistic: 10 Tips for Teenagers with Asperger Syndrome or 'Mild' Autism." Autistic, Not Weird. N.p., 2016. Web. 24 Mar. 2016.

Carpenter, Siri. "Disconnected: Adults with Autism Are Left Alone to Navigate a Jarring World." Science News 187.4 (2015): 16-20. Web.

Ford, Ian, and Stephanie Hamilton. "A Field Guide to Earthlings." Albuquerque, NM: Ian Ford Software Corporation, 2010. Print.

Kim, Cynthia. "Adult Diagnosis." Musings of an Aspie. N.p., 2016. Web. 24 Mar. 2016.

Willey, Liane Holliday. "Pretending To Be Normal." London: Jessica Kingsley, 1999. Print.

Author Bios

John M. Harpster

John M. Harpster was born in Ft. Worth, Texas and raised in Arlington. After several years of odd jobs, he went back to college and got his bachelor's degree in Computer Science from California State University in Northridge, CA. His first job after college was in Fort Worth, Texas at General Dynamics. He met and started dating Tamara Stensland, also a software engineer at General Dynamics, and they were married in Dallas, Texas. Before the birth of their son he wrote articles for a computer magazine but put that aside when he became the father of an autistic boy. He and his family live in Lakeside, California with their son John.

John returned to writing with his debut book of the Dancing with the Universe Series, "Doing the E.T. Tango". He is working on additional books for the Dancing with the Universe series and other ideas. He is currently writing on other books, including another satire called "Elijah". He is also building a wooden robot that he can put in the front seat of his car to enable him to drive in the HOV lanes on the freeway.

Tamara Harpster

Tamara Harpster was born December 5, 1962, which is also Walt Disney's birthday and the day Mozart died, two facts she has been trying to reconcile ever since she found them out. Her childhood was spent in various cities in the Midwest as her family moved around for her father's job. After graduating from Oklahoma State University she got her first job and met her husband to be on her first project. They married a year later and are still together some 30 years later. In that time she has been a software engineer, motel owner/manager, web developer, project manager and is currently part owner of another small business. In her spare time she works with her husband John to polish up his novels, and do her own writing for blog entries and essays. She is working on a fantasy series "Hero Lottery" and a science fiction novel "Year 2038 Bug". The book "Year 2038 Bug" will be published as a serial on their website.

Thank you for reading *"You Don't Want to Go For a Ride.* We would appreciate it if you would leave a review for the book on the site where you bought it. Your feedback is important for us and for other readers.

Our website contains blog articles by Tamara about autism and life in the country. We also announce new books on the site and offer previews of our upcoming books.

Interested in more books and articles from Shell Creek Publishing?

Follow us on Facebook or Twitter, or check out our web page.

Facebook - http://www.facebook.com/shellcreekbooks

Shell Creek Publishing - http://www.shellcreekpublishing.com

@shellcreekbooks on Twitter - https://twitter.com/shellcreekbooks

While formatting the book, John-John asked me to include pictures from a story he drew many years ago. There are no words with any of his illustrations but it appears to be a story about a smiley face and a heart as they travel together somewhere. These two pictures seemed a good way to end our book.

Tamara

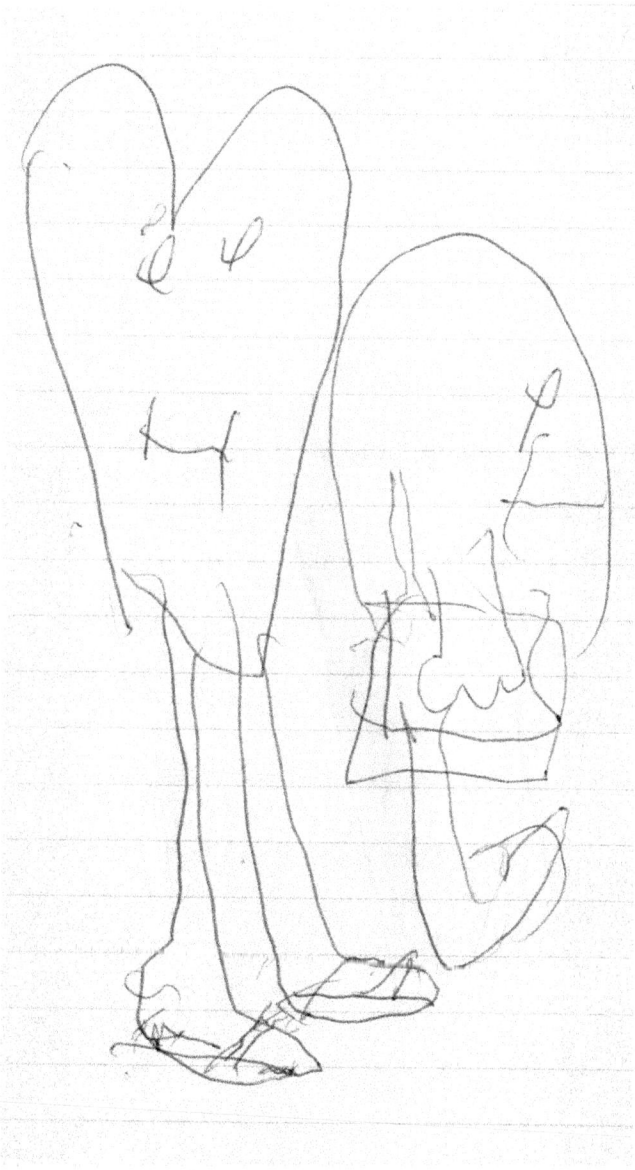

www.ingramcontent.com/pod-product-compliance
Lightning Source LLC
Chambersburg PA
CBHW021826090426
42811CB00032B/2044/J